How To

MW00781018

Like A Book

The Complete Guide To Analyze People, Decode

Emotions, Predict Intentions, Behavior, And

Connect Effortlessly

Jason Williams

TABLE OF CONTENT

Introduction 5

The Psychology of Human Behavior

PART - II

The Art of Reading People

PART - III

Communication and Social Interaction

INTRODUCTION

Have you ever wondered what it would be like to have a relationship where you are thoroughly understood and have no problems understanding the next person? Would you like to skip the drama of needing to weed out insincere people from your circle of friends without having to waste extended periods in such relationships? Are you having trouble understanding the intentions behind people's actions or even the things that they say? Do you frequently find yourself in a situation where people say one thing and expect you to do something else because there is an unspoken understanding that they did communicate this "something else" to you? All of this sounded very confusing, right?

If you answered yes to any of these, this book in your hand would help you sort through the chaos of your relationships and put you on track to understanding people better. When you think about the relationships you have lost and the ones you wish you could have, one common trend you would find is guilt attached to regrets about the things you want to you could have said or the ability to take back the things you said. This guilt is not restricted to your role in those relationships. It also includes a conflict of interest and desire to understand what the other person really wants or, at the very least, what they are saying. At the end of the day, you arrive at one conclusion, which is…everything comes back to communication. So, what exactly is communication, and how important is it in the relationships that we build?

Before I answer that question, I want to approach this from a very personal angle. I am sure you know that there is truly little more disappointing than failure to thrive in your relationship with people. Whether it is with family, friends, or colleagues at work, that failure makes you feel like an outsider. It has a way of stripping you of your confidence and leaving you with a strong sense of disappointment. This used to be me, and at some point, in my life, I would sit in the corner and declare that I had no place in this world, and for a while, I was comfortable in this illusion I created for myself. I even deceived myself into believing that I was comfortable being the outsider. But you know the thing with illusions, at some point, you must confront the reality of things, and the truth is that we need people in our lives.

Humans are created for interaction and relations. However, communication is what establishes those relationships. Not bond, not obligation not even filial affiliations; simply good old fashion communication. My turnaround story happened after I suffered a major disappointment in life. I was overlooked for promotion in office, which broke me deeply because I worked hard for it. At this point, I realized that the world isn't just going to hand you things simply because you deserve it even though you have worked hard for it. It is crucial that we learn to communicate our needs. However, in communicating our feelings, we must also learn not to offend the people we are communicating with. It is one thing to be articulate. It is another thing to be offensive because you can equally end up isolating yourself from people in that process.

Communication is key to the survival of any kind of relationship. Through communication, you can understand your shared values, expectations, and, most significantly, the boundaries of that relationship. In this current day and age, a lot of people struggle with this fundamental aspect of socialization. Beyond what is being said verbally, there are many non-verbal cues with essential messages that can fly over your head if you do not pay attention to them. Unfortunately, the art of communication is buried under all the multiple mixed messages streamed directly to our homes via multiple sources, making it incredibly difficult to make sense of the world around us today. This is further complicated by the age of digital living that allows you to forge relationships with many people at once. This sounds fantastic on the surface, but the pressure that comes from finding love at a swipe and living up to the expectations of people who do not even know your last name creates pressure that makes it even harder to connect with people authentically.

This book chronicles my journey from that place of social awkwardness to becoming the kind of person people actually want to spend time around. In it, I share the lessons I learned in the process and also practical principles that you can implement in your everyday communication to make life that much more interesting. So yes, you may be feeling disappointed now. People may have let you down, but it does not mean the end.

If I have learned anything in life, it is this; disappointment is a signal that you are moving into a new phase. An end is simply a new beginning. So, keep an open mind. You may need to change certain habits. This does not essentially mean you have to change things about yourself. It is more of changing your perspective on things and then learning to become a little more assertive. Less than six months later, after applying the knowledge I gained, I was able to get that promotion, and ever since then, I have kept growing. Not just in my workplace, but in my relationships with people as well. And so, I am genuinely excited to share these experiences with you in the hopes that your life takes a positive turn from here on out. From now on, always remind yourself that you have the power to transform your life. Not your boss, not your partner, not your parents. The authority has always been in your hands. You just need to understand how to wield it.

This book is created as a manual to help you decode people in a short time. So, whether you are having an actual face to face conversation, face-timing your pals on social media, or having over the phone chats, you can use subtle signals such as voice inflections, body language, and even facial expressions. At the end of each chapter, you would find exercises that help you take positive actions towards achieving your relationship goals. I believe that putting the knowledge that you gain into practice is the best way to get you closer to the results that you want in your life. I hope that this book gives you everything that you desire and then some more. Here's to wonderful new beginnings!

Having said that, let us get started by exploring why people act the way that they do.

Part One

The Psychology of Human Behavior

Chapter One

WHY DO WE ACT THE WAY THAT WE DO?

Human behavior is one of the most puzzling things ever. Often, it appears that we do things randomly without giving any thought to why we do or say the things that we do. Science, however, tells us otherwise. Those seemingly chaotic out-of-nowhere actions are driven by something deep within us that we may not even understand or be aware of. From your sleeping patterns to the way you interact with people, there is a logical explanation of why we act the way we do. There is still a lot of debate regarding people cultivating years of habits that dictate their actions and people who are simply born the way they are.

In this chapter, our primary focus is going to be on the things that we can explain. This is because when you understand why people do the things that they do, you are in a better position to figure out those grey areas that are usually present in the communication style of most relationships. From looking at what motivates people to explore how our gender (whether chosen or assigned) impacts our way of life, one thing is sure—understanding the "why" helps you understand the "what" of everything. And when you get to this place, figuring people out becomes an easier task.

The Five Things that Motivate Our Actions

Motivation is a mental driving force that keeps you on track with your goals and actions. It is essentially the "why" behind what we do. In general, there are so many motivating factors for each of us. Some of them are internal, and some are external. The internal motivators have you staying motivated by internal factors like your desire to achieve certain milestones and so on.

On the other hand, external motivators are factors outside of you, like other people's expectations. But in this segment, I want us to look at five crucial factors that drive our behavior. I chose to focus on these five because they cut across gender, race, social status, and even religion.

Power Motivation:

This type of motivation is about control. It involves the need to stay in charge, which influences your communication style, which in turn dictates the role you play in relationships— this kind of motivation type used to be predominant in men. But as the world pushes for gender equality, it is safe to say that anyone could have power and the need for control as their trigger switch. A person who is driven by power motivation tends to take an aggressive stance in their non-verbal communication. On the positive side, this makes them solution-oriented and more interested in changing their world positively. On the negative side, they can be driven to extreme lengths to manipulate people and circumstances so that they can stay in control.

Achievement Motivation:

The possession of material things can be an excellent motivational force if you focus on the right things. Here, a person is motivated by getting their goals, crossing off their to-do lists, and checking the milestone boxes. People whose actions are driven by achievement motivation can sometimes be regarded as materialistic. But as I mentioned earlier, this is only possible if they focus on the wrong things. When you understand what motivates this person, you will discover that these people are very visual and like to have a chart that records their process and determines their progress. Their communication style is usually more assertive than aggressive because they know to have a strong knowledge of what they want.

Reward Motivation:

This is kind of like achievement motivation as there is also a visual element to this. However, the significant difference lies in the process that leads to the end goal. Reward motivation is like a carrot that is dangled at the mouth of the rabbit's hole to draw it out. People motivated by rewards typically have a "what's-in-it-for-me" attitude, and this can make them appear selfish. This strongly influences Their communication style, whether verbal or non-verbal. As with every type of motivation, you have people on two extremes. You have those who use reward to push their actions. These people can successfully turn their reward into an achievement, which means they work with a plan for their process. On the other extreme, you have people who are willing to do anything, including compromise their integrity to get what they want. Drug addicts and gamblers are often motivated by reward.

Fear-Based Motivation:

Like it or not, fear is a powerful motivator, and its influence can be negative or positive. The impact of fear-based motivation is determined by your attitude towards. Some people can channel their emotions and use them as the fuel that pushes them towards their goals. This does not in any way mean that they have overcome their fears. It is an indication that instead of allowing the fear to cripple them, they turn it into the wind beneath their wings. Those who do not channel their fear the right way would often use it to escape the thing that scares them. In their non-verbal communication, you would find cues that highlight their insecurities and fragile emotional state. You should know about people who are motivated by fear because they are in no way weak or timid person. Their fear sometimes forces them to make radical decisions, and this, among other things, makes them unpredictable.

Competence Motivation:

This is a motivational factor driven by the need to be better. Athletes and people in a competitive environment are usually spurred on by competence. They want to see themselves evolve for the better to find that they are always pushing themselves. Like people motivated by achievements, they like to work with a plan and can be both aggressive and assertive in their communication style. You would hardly ever find them sitting around doing nothing. Their enthusiasm for getting things done can be both infectious and intimidating at the same time. When you meet a person like this, you are forced to step up your game or, at the very least, sit up straighter. Laziness is something that they have very little tolerance for.

Four Main Personality Types Based on Temperaments

If you have been looking around the internet for questions about people's personality or even your own, chances are you have already come across these temperament types. In this segment, I am going to go over the main temperament types without going in-depth on them just to help you get an understanding of what you already know and also show you how this can play into the way people communicate and relate with you. It is also important to note that no one is limited to just one type of temperament. We are all made of a blend of at least two characters. However, there will be one temperament type that will be dominant. If you are new to all of this, I suggest you put a page marker here and do a little bit of internet research on the subject to make the most of the information that will be shared in this chapter.

Temperament Type One: Sanguine

The sanguine guy or girl is that lively, boisterous person who always seems to know everybody when they walk into a room. Most people describe them as fun-loving and people-oriented. It is difficult and almost impossible to stay down around a sanguine person because their buoyant nature would immediately draw you out of your gloomy shell. In communication, they tend to talk a lot. If you are looking for cues in their communication, a lot of it would be found in what they say because of their talkative nature. Their natural charisma, innate joie de vivre, and personal charm can make anyone feel so warm and connected that they can almost talk themselves out of any situation.

Temperament Type Two: Choleric

This is another extroverted character, but they are nowhere near the people with sanguine temperament. They are practical, opinionated to the point of being stubborn and have no problems making decisions for themselves and you. A choleric guy is a type that would take a girl on a date and order for himself and her as well without batting an eyelid. While he shares some of the extroverted traits of the sanguine, he is not as emotional. You would be right if you said a choleric guy sees emotion as weakness. But to make up for this emotional defect, a person with a choleric temperament does more action than talking. While the sanguine person is busy telling you how they plan to build their future, the choleric is actually out there in the trenches working out the plans they have made to make their dreams a reality.

Temperament Type Three: Melancholy

Have you ever met those artsy types who seem to have their faces pinched in a painful expression whenever they observe an art piece at a showing? You know. The kind that can analyze a single spherical red dot on a white canvass and interpret it most philosophically? Yep. That person most likely has a melancholic temperament. Do not let this word's negative connotation fool you into thinking that these are one of those darker personalities. While they tend to be broody, contemplative, and extremely sensitive, these people are usually very gifted. They are emotionally intuitive, the least selfish of all the temperaments, and very loyal to the few people they call friends. The major problem would be getting them to know you well enough to call you their friend. Clues as to their true state of mind would be in facial expressions that can be exaggerated sometimes and their words, which can also have a double meaning.

Temperament Type Four: Phlegmatic

These are your calm and easy-going types. They are not exactly the party every weekend type, but you would not find them desperately clinging to walls at the event. Everybody loves them because they are cool, calm, and slow to anger. They enjoy their own company from time to time, but they also thrive in a community. They are the thoughtful neighbors who will help water your yard if they see it getting brown without creating a fuss about it or making you feel guilty. On the flip side, the phlegmatic tend to be too laid back in their approach to life. That is not to say that if they are thrust into a position that requires action, you will find them lacking. They would just not put themselves upfront for it. In communication, they do not always share their true feelings. You would need to pay attention to body language and facial expressions to understand what they are hiding behind the mask.

Now that we have looked at all four personality types, I would like to remind you that nobody is ever just one personality type through and through. You could be a SAN-MEL, a CHLOR-PHLEG, and in some cases, there could be three personalities in varying ratios present in a person. There are cases where a person could be 45% Mel, 35%Chlor and 20% San. But whatever category you fall into, you would find that there is one personality that stands out. This is usually referred to as your dominant personality. There are personality tests that you can take to help determine what your dominant personality is. Also, your upbringing and social background could determine how your personality finds expression.

Three Types of People You Should Avoid

Every personality type has its unique trait, flaws, and strengths. But there are people who embody specific characteristics that make it nearly impossible to build a healthy relationship with them. If you have ever encountered such people, you will find yourself using toxic, negative, and unpleasant words to describe what you had with them. No matter how well these people hide their true nature, the red flags they put out there should never be ignored. This book is about reading people better to be in a better position to build good relationships. I firmly believe that I would fail in my duty if I do not write this mini relationship blacklist. You must understand that changing people or fixing them is not your responsibility. The only thing you are obligated to do is understand them and make yourself understood, hence, the book in your hand.

When you come across people who act like anyone on this list, you must immediately accept that the best thing you can do for them and let them go.

1. The Manipulator:

These people are good at twisting every situation, event, or spoken word into a narrative that supports their perspectives and objectives. For them, it is more about getting what they want than anything else. Their manipulative strategies include the use of gaslighting and lies. Anyone who invests that much negative energy to get you to do something that you probably would not have done on an average day would only get worse as their relationship with you progresses. A manipulator's impact on your mental health is quite devasting as you would find yourself feeling incompetent in things that you are usually adept at. Your self-esteem would be at an all-time low, and there would be moments where you question your mental health and sanity.

All in all, avoid manipulators. They are no good for you. One of the red flags that indicates the person you are communicating with has manipulative tendencies is the condescending way they speak to people. Manipulators think that they are better than everyone else, and they cannot mask it in their speech.

2. The Controller

Being a little controlling is not bad. People with this trait tend to get things done on time with their goal-getting attitude. But when a person extends their need for control to someone else's life, be it child, spouse, or employee, you are bound to have a lot of issues. Controlling people start as manipulators. They employ the same tricks as the manipulator to make you do what they want. When they see that you still have a mind of your own, they might resort to physical means, which usually ends in violence. In today's world that we live in, no relationship justifies violence or abuse in any form. There are many ways for people to show that they care, but violence for any reason is not one of them. If you find yourself in a violent relationship, you need to get yourself out. Why? Because you deserve better. A controlling person tries to hide their despicable deeds under the guise of "doing what is best for you." They want you to think that no one else can love you or care for you as they do. The moment you buy into what they are "selling," they sort of own you.

3. The 24/7 Downer

There are moments in our lives when we will feel as though the battle we are fighting on this journey called life is us versus the rest of the world. But the 24/7 downer takes this feeling to a whole new level. It is almost as if the very air that they breathe is made of pure toxic energy. The sun could be shining outside in all its brilliance and glory, but the downer would only feel thunderstorms and rain clouds. These people love to complain and play the victim role. Their negative attitude produces toxic fumes that will curdle any sign of positivity. Your happiness and progress in life would be interpreted as a symbol of doom for them. Their only source of joy sees you just as miserable as they are. One significant trait of a 24/7 downer out of many is their innate ability to assign blame to anyone and everyone except themselves. Relationships are meant to help you evolve into a better version of yourself. Anything less is just not worth it.

The Duality of Our Nature: Masculine and Feminine

Regardless of our chosen or biological gender, each of us has a dual nature that speaks to our capacity to connect and build relationships. This is not about the socially assigned traits of being male or female. It is about exploring your true nature and expectations in relationships. When you connect with your real personality without thinking about gender, people who appreciate you will reciprocate. At the end of the day, you will have a stable relationship that satisfies your social needs. Female friendships tend to have a more emotional template to them, while male companies are more physical. But some men crave emotional connections in their friendships and women who wished their girls pals were more into physical activities like hiking in the woods rather than discussing their latest relationship escapades over cocktails.

This duality of nature within us is part of what motivates our actions, especially when dealing with other people. When you bring all these elements together (core beliefs, driving force, personality type, and then our dual nature), what you get is a behind-the-scenes sneak peek into people's minds. With that preview, you can be a little more forgiving with the shortfalls and mistakes people make. You will probably learn to appreciate the people that you have in your life genuinely. That communication barrier that seems to make forging relationships difficult would come down and offer opportunities at establishing stronger bonds.

Just have it at the back of your mind that this is not going to happen overnight. There are a million other things to consider but understanding that necessary background information on human behavior is the first step. Get it right, and the rest of the chapters in the book would make sense. Having said this, before you run off to start trying to figure people out, the first place to start is with you. You are one of the key characters in any type of relationship that you have. To know what gets you up in the morning, what motivates you, what excites you, and even what gets you down is a huge deal. Hopefully, the content of this chapter can help you to start asking the right questions. With that in mind, put things in motion by completing the exercise below.

Exercise

After reading the first part, take a moment to ask yourself why you do the things that you do. If that sounds too complicated, start with your reason for buying this book. Beyond the problem that it solves, what exactly are you craving in relationships, and why are you craving it? Write your answers down in a journal, and then see if you can figure out what motivates you.

If you are not sure what your temperament type is, take this short quiz

1. Are you an extrovert? Yes or No?

If yes, you are probably sanguine or choleric. If not, you are most likely melancholic or phlegmatic.

2. In a room full of people, are you usually the first to speak? Yes or No?

If yes to one and two, you are more sanguine than choleric.

3. Do you thrive naturally in leadership positions? Yes or No?

If you responded yes to one and no to two, then you are leaning towards choleric.

4. Do you tend to overanalyze, criticize and push for perfection? Yes or No?

If you answered no to 1, 2, and 3 but yes to 4, you might be melancholic.

5. Are you often described as quiet, peaceful but kind of a pushover? Yes or No?

If yes, your dominant personality might be phlegmatic.

This mini quiz will only show you what your dominant temperament is. To uncover your full temperament ratio, you would need to carry out a more extensive test online. But before you approach these quizzes, you must make deliberate efforts to get rid of the mindset that one temperament is better than the other simply because you desire it. All temperaments have their negatives and positives, strengths, and weaknesses. No temperament is all-around perfect. Keep an open mind and be accepting of the outcome. Accepting yourself for who you are, gives yourself the chance to grow into who you want to become.

Chapter Two

HUMAN INTERACTION IN THE DIGITAL AGE

The rise and rise of the internet have opened a lot of possibilities for everyone. People who otherwise would have been trapped in the small world surrounding them have now been given access to a much bigger platform. From the comfort of your bed, you can place an order for a product 2 continents away, have it shipped to a client, conduct a group meeting with people physically present in 6 different countries, flirt with 10 different strangers and all of this before you are done with your first cup of coffee. While all of this sounds great, there have been some major setbacks because of this. Communication has become even more difficult even though we have all these tremendous messaging apps designed for this purpose specifically. It is difficult to understand why many people feel cut off from the world even though they are on socializing platforms that connect them with billions of other people. You might think the ideal thing to do is completely disconnect yourself from social media. This might temporarily help you get yourself together mentally, but the best line of action is to understand the virtual world and how to thrive in it. Learn to distinguish between what is fake and what is real. Decode the true personality behind the person you are chatting with online and create connections with real people. In this chapter, I am going to be breaking down this process in the simplest way.

Social Media and its Impact on Today's Culture

As I mentioned in the introduction to this chapter, social media is something that we cannot do without. Like it or not, it is a powerful communication tool if you know how to use it. But without proper usage, it can easily become a source of distress and anxiety. The pandemic, which mandated that a lot of people work from home, has made it become a necessity. The success of that process has been because of the presence of social media. Another area where you can see the impact is in the drive for social justice. Through social media, the voices of people calling for change have been amplified, which has spurred the government into taking prompt positive actions to remedy the situation. If we delve more into the subject, we could spend the rest of this book discussing social media's impact, but I am more interested in how all of this affects you as an individual.

For starters, you are introduced to people who you probably would never have met otherwise. Now because we know that communication in person can be very tricky, we assume that the anonymity that social media provides should make it easier, right?

Wrong. There is a whole new set of rules that you need to follow if you want to make sense of anything happening there. And get this, each social media platform has its own set of rules if you're going to thrive. For example, Twitter has a limited number of characters you can use in each message, so if you have a lot to say, you have to learn to curate your message so that people can understand you better. Instagram, on the other hand, is a visual platform. A picture they say is worth a thousand words. Still, here, it could be worth one connection or 1 million connections depending on the quality of the image and your application/integration of the platform's algorithms.

There is also the misguided notion that we must be on all social media platforms and keep up with what everyone else is doing. This puts an additional strain on communication and makes it difficult to find our individual authentic voices, so we end up sounding just like everyone else. Now, this is where the main problem in communication begins. Because you no longer have your own voice, your relationship needs to end up being sacrificed, and when this happens, you will find yourself in a lot of fake relationships. The fake social media life presents a challenge when you are trying to make genuine connections. As if these problems were not enough, social media has made it extremely possible for people to live a double life, which is the opposite of what they have in the real world. So, with all these challenges, how can you sieve through the rubble to establish genuine connections?

This whole chapter is dedicated to answering that question, but as with everything that has to do with relationships, the first place to start is with yourself. Decide on what you want on social media. If you just want to cruise along with everyone else without needing to make long-lasting connections, you can set up an online persona, build an identity around this persona and perhaps create a brand out of it. However, if connecting with real people for real relationships, whether for friendships, love, or business, you would have to make a deliberate effort to be real and stay true to who you are and whatever your expectations may be. I personally believe that the energy you put out there will come back to you. In addition to that, there are additional steps you can take to simplify your online communications.

Virtual Personality Vs. Reality

The first rule of social media is to take what you find there with a grain of salt. In other words, do not take it so seriously. These days, terminologies like clout chasing, going viral, among many others become a part of the digital world. The need to get attention in the form of likes, shares, and retweets has caused a lot of people to take extreme measures like posting sensational content that is meant to shock their followers. But if you meet them in real life, you will find that the online persona and the antics carried out by that persona have next to nothing in common with their real self. Some people are so invested in the illusion that they have created online that they go the extra length to fabricate details about this person. When you hear about romance/dating scam, you would hear stories about how these fictional men/women inspired so much love and devotion that their victims were willing to part with huge sums of money, in some cases, their life savings without ever having to meet this person physically only to find out that the person that they have been talking to all the while does not even exist.

The second rule of communication via social media is never making any serious decisions until you have established some kind of physical connection. If you are going to send money to anyone, do not do it because of a sob story said to you via chats. At least agree to a public sit down with this person. If the distance is a problem, have a consistent voice and video calls with this person for some months before taking things any further. This person may be telling you the right stuff, painting themselves in the most perfect way, and generally making you feel like all your dreams have come true. But the fact is this, as long as all of that is online, there is still an extraordinarily strong possibility that everything has been fabricated. More than that, you must understand that it is easy to manipulate people online. You do not have the luxury of reading their facial expressions or taking other cues from their body language. The only thing you have from your conversations and communications with them to rely on is what they choose to reveal to you.

Now do not get me wrong. There have been a lot of instances where people have been able to defy these irregularities and still build a stable relationship that transitioned from the online space into real life. But do not get sucked into thinking that those relationships were just chance happenings that led to something serious. There is a lot of vetting that has to be undergone just so that the individuals involved get to a place where they can trust each other enough to make a real-life commitment. Before you get into the process of vetting a person, there are subtle clues that you can use to determine their personality or character in reality, and I am going to share this in the next segment.

Unmasking the Person Behind the Avatar

So, you have met this person online. It doesn't matter if this platform is a dating site or a regular social media handle. The main question on your mind is how to really figure out who this person is. Before we go any further, let me remind you that these tips are not 100% foolproof. However, you can weed out unsavory characters, which depending on the platform, and the circumstance, could be a lot. Having said that, let us begin.

1. Pay attention to the profile.

A business account is a clear sign that the owner of that account is interested in business dealings. People carrying out personal actions on social media with their business accounts is a red flag. Not only is it unprofessional, but it also calls their business ethics to question. If you intend to carry out business dealings with this account, ensure that you conduct extensive background research before you do so. If the profile of the person you are engaging with belongs to a personal account, look for details like their bio. Personal accounts with little to no information speak to an account owner that is trying to remain inconspicuous. This in itself is not a crime. But it could also be an indicator of something fishy, especially after you read the next tip.

2. Carefully assess the content that they put out.

While you should have it in the back of your mind that the content that people put on social media platforms does not always reflect the account owner's personal opinions in real life, it is quite possible that there are some sinister motives behind the content. Some people put up sexually explicit images so that they can lure unsuspecting victims. The general term for this catfishing. Sexually appealing photos are not the only way people try to scam and manipulate victims online. Fraudulent business entities tend to post exaggerated testimonials attesting to the effectiveness of their products. They also put-up financial figures with falsified data or claims in the hopes that it would appeal to greedy investors. These clues are not always so straightforward if you approach these types of accounts without awareness. Some fraudulent businesses have mastered the ability to doctor their social media content so professionally that it is hard to suspect them. In that situation, you should check out the next tip.

3. Look into how long that account has been in existence.

We are living in a digital age. Unless you are totally living off the grid, you must somehow have a virtual footprint. An account that suddenly pops out and immediately starts putting up catfishing content is definitely suspicious. Whether they are trying to bait prospective dates or investors, the modus operandi is quite similar. Accounts with sinister intentions try too hard to make themselves appear authentic.

If you find yourself being suspicious of an account, go over the three tips I have just listed, and if they check all three, you might want to suspend all engagements with such accounts until you can verify their authenticity. Now that you have gotten past the initial issues with vetting the account, the next step is getting to know the account's personality. Here, I am going to share clues that you can use to unmask the person behind the account even before you meet with them.

i. Their diction

The English language is commonly used in most forms of communication. I would not go as far as calling it the most universal language, but it comes pretty close as you would find records of it spoken in almost every country. Being universal does not mean that everybody says it in the same way. If the person you are communicating with speaks English, one of the first things you should do is determine where they are from. Then pay attention to the way they say. If their accent or written texts do not correspond with the location that they give you, chances are, the person is either deliberately misleading you or making a poor attempt to impress you, which is just as bad. Also, in line with this, a person who says they are educated is going to be more fluent in their communication skills. However, there might be instances where the person obtained their degree in a foreign language.

ii. Ghosting

This is a word to describe the action of just disappearing from plans or commitments made with people without any prior notice. People who make it a habit of disappearing after planning a video call or other events with you are giving you clear indications that they are insincere. Usually, they come up with seemingly sound excuses for their abrupt disappearances. This time around, do not pay attention to what they are saying. Focus instead on their actions. When you communicate with this person, do you find that you can only reach them at odd hours? This is especially suspicious if you are on an online dating forum and the person tells you that they are single. No matter how busy a person is, they should be able to prioritize their time for the person they are seeing.

iii. Inconsistent stories

The thing about telling lies is that you have to reveal even more lies in order to keep up with the initial lie. When this continues, you will discover that you have spurned a web of lies so tangled and complicated that you end up becoming trapped in them. This is what happens with deceitful people. In the beginning, their stories might make sense and seem plausible. But with time, those stories would begin to crumble. Now time is the one thing you may not have. After all, who wants to waste time trying to figure out if a person is fake or not? From the onset, a person who approaches you with extraordinary tales of woe and tragedy within a week of meeting you might at best be someone who has lived through some tough times but enjoy using their tragic circumstances to elicit sympathy. This will then be used to manipulate you. At worst, the person is laying the groundwork for the requests they will make of you later.

Avoiding the Filtered Life

On social media, you can doctor a picture to look absolutely perfect but nothing like the original. There are contouring tools that can be used to create abs, Kim Kardashian style butt, and skin so smooth that there is not a single blemish. But when you meet the person in real life, what you find would be a whole different ball game entirely. Can you do anything to stop this? Not really? I mean, at the end of the day, you want to put your best foot forward and present a side of you that you feel is the most appealing. So, yes. You might doctor that photo a little. Turn the lights all the way up until you find just the right level for you. If you have the suitable devices, you might be able to airbrush some scars away, edit some unpleasant features and enhance your attributes. Does this make you a bad person? No. Just don't overdo it to the point where you are unrecognizable.

However, when dealing with other people, it might be better not to attach your connection to them based on your attraction to certain physical attributes. Beyond the alteration of appearance using software, there are things that can be done to give an illusion of perfection. People without hair buy extensions. Getting blue eyes, a beard, and ample bosom is no longer something that you leave to genetics. A quick trip to your local vendor can change the game for you. Because of this fact, trying to determine a person's background based on their appearance can be likened to judging a book by its cover. Is there any way to escape the filtered life? As long as you are dealing with social media, the answer is no. So, what do you then do about it?

My advice to you is to focus on the real stuff. Nothing can beat the old-fashioned way of communication which is why the rest of the book is dedicated to managing real-time communication with people. If there is any major lesson, I would like you to take away from this chapter, it would be the fact that nothing is ever as it seems in the world of virtual reality. Can you build strong and authentic relationships in the virtual world, yes? But it takes discipline and attention to detail to separate the real from the fake. If you are willing to put in the extra amount of work, put your head before your heart and make safe decisions, you should be just fine. Personally, I feel that social media presents a perfect no-pressure situation to help you practice and learn the basics of human interaction. On a final note, always remember to take everything with a pinch of salt. Graciously accept the compliments without attaching any significant meaning to it and viciously ignore the negative comments even though they make your blood boil. Keep it classy and civil but always keep it real.

Exercise

1. Conduct an audit of all your social media accounts. Look at the platforms where you are most active and the ones where you are least active.

2. For those accounts where you are most active, as yourself, what are the things you have posted about? What conversations have you participated in? How would you rate your experience on these platforms, and how much have they impacted you physically, emotionally, and mentally?

3. For the accounts where you are least active, find out why you are holding on to them. If you cannot find any tangible reason to stay on the platform, deactivate and let go.

4. At this point, you should have a fairly good idea about the accounts you are going to hold on to. Take your journal and write down what you hope to get out of your social experience.

5. When you have completed steps 1 to 4, you are ready to do social media on your own terms. Just ensure that your actions and the people you connect with aligning with what you have written down in number 4.

On a final note, I urge you to let go of any assumptions you may have about anyone on social media. This can lead to disappointments and, in some cases, hamper your ability to connect with said persons. Also, try to ensure that your real life doesn't revolve around social media. Be firm about the boundaries you set and take extra precautions before taking a social media relationship offline. And no matter what some negative social media personalities may say about you, remind yourself that you are the only one who can really define who you are. Now that we have completed our talk about managing communication through social media let us look at some of those wise sayings that sound like the actual logical explanation but end up being myths about our behavior.

Chapter Three

FACTS, MYTHS AND COMMON MISCONCEPTIONS ABOUT HUMAN BEHAVIOR

After looking at the things that motivate our actions and exploring how you can navigate the world of digital living, it makes sense that our next stop would be clearing up those misconceptions and assumptions you have about human behavior. Some of these myths are socially ingrained in us via our upbringing. Some are things that we just pick up in our environment. There are some of those notions that were gotten through a negative experience. For example, a woman who was cheated on and betrayed by someone she loved, trusted, and planned to spend a future with can come out of that situation with the notion that all men are scum. While we know that there are some men who have definitely earned their scum badge, there are still a lot of amazing ones. But carrying this kind of mindset can negatively impact this woman's ability to genuinely connect with a man. In this chapter, I would like to shatter those stereotypes about human behavior and help you get into your next relationship that is built on truths and healthy expectations.

The Lies We Tell Other People

Right now, the world is having what I like to call an 'identity crisis.' There are so many labels flying around. Many definitions of what we think we should be and how we think we should act; so many societal expectations. In other words, there are so many voices telling us who they think we should be. This is even amplified by the fact that the world is now a global village, and technology has made it possible for us to connect with people across continents at the touch of a button. And so, with all these millions of voices screaming at us at the speed of light, we have failed to pay attention to the one voice that matters the most: our voice. Well, no more. In this chapter, I am going to share some of the things we say that set the tone for the relationship without even knowing it.

1. Your Relationship is Made up of the Other Person

There is one simple fact in any social interaction that involves you; you make up half of that relationship. For some reason, we always forget this fact and choose to work with the

41

untruth that the other person must be the one to do something. Suppose you are constantly sitting around waiting for the things you desire in a relationship to happen through the next person's spoken words or actions. In that case, you will end up disappointed and unsatisfied. If you fancy a person, work up the courage and talk to them. It may not always yield a positive outcome, but at least you would know that you have effectively played your part. If you want a position in your office, do not secretly wish for it. Let your intentions be known, and then put in the work that will help you achieve them.

2. It is okay

These three words are the most spoken in any relationship. And when it comes to dealing with people, we use this as a mask to hide the extent of our true feelings. When you mask your emotions, you take away an opportunity to get to the heart of a problem. This is because you have filed away your true emotions under the misguided notion of wanting to keep the peace. When a person does something that hurts or negatively affects you, telling them it is okay in the face of your pain trivializes their actions and your feelings. And trust me, under these circumstances, you will not be able to read their countenance. The effort that you spend bottling up those emotions will blind you to the reality of things. The next lie explains why a lot of us do this.

3. We are not good enough

Back in my days at this firm, I knew I desired this managing position at work. I put in the work and put in the time for it. But every time I was passed over, I justified it by saying the other party was more deserving of the job because I was not good enough. This lie also played out in my romantic relationships. Whenever I got dumped, I would shove the pain deep down and tell myself that the other person was better. Even when I finally got into this magnificent relationship that was everything I desired, I sabotaged it because I did not think I deserved it. Many people who always seem to be repeating the "shitty" relationship cycle are trapped in it because of this lie here. This is a major blinder as it blocks you from seeing the person you are in a relationship with, not their good or their bad. It just focuses on your incompetence.

4. People's opinions are more important

It would be impossible to read people if your personal opinions are buried under other people's opinions. There are certain social cliches designed to curb our individual voices. My least favorite is the one about leaning on the experiences of other people if you have none. To some extent, this might make sense, but we have something called intuition for the most part. Some of the best interrogators and police investigators rely on their training and gut to effectively do their jobs. Their experiences come from learning to follow their instincts. Dealing with people comes from an instinctual path. Whenever you meet a person, you would have an instant reaction to the person. People may have an opinion about the said person, but your instinct relays information that should not be ignored.

5. I can never...

When you believe that you cannot do something, chances are, you will not do it. In communication, these words are powerful enough to keep you in the dark about people's true nature. This is because the words themselves are very self-limiting. When you have passed a vote of no confidence in yourself, you will end up seeking validation elsewhere, which more often than not ends up being in the wrong places people. When you seek validation from people, you immediately put-on blinders that keep you from seeing the person for who they really are. If you take away a single message from this book, let it be this: You are capable of more than you can imagine. Second, guessing yourself will invalidate your intuitions, trivialize your opinions, dim your perspective and keep you from building healthy relationships.

The Truths that We Must Keep to Ourselves

Telling lies in any relationship is like digging at the foundations of a house. You take away the very thing on which the relationship stands on which is trust. Still, some truths are better kept to yourself. Ethically, we feel obligated to disclose every single truth in a relationship, but when you are in the business of trying to figure people out, some truths will shut the door of opportunity in your face before you get the chance to make something out of that relationship. I want you to have it at the back of your mind that we are looking at building a relationship with someone you just met in this context.

Many of us may have the urge to lay all our cards on the table to know where we stand, or at least the other person knows where they stand with us, and while this notion is applaudable, it does not always have good consequences. This is because people are naturally judgmental in nature. So, when you lay open with these truths, you make it difficult for the other person to open themselves to you or to look at the possibility of getting to know you outside these things. I am not saying you should never tell people these things but wait until your relationship has progressed to a certain level before you unveil your truth. Having said that, here is a list of things you just have to keep to yourself.

1. Your insecurities

When you make your insecurity your first order of business in any conversation, you amplify that voice of low self-esteem that you already have, which will go on to reduce your confidence. Sociologists say this is because even though this person is completely accepting of you and your flaws, you would always have it at the back of your mind that they know something about you that you feel can be used against you. So, suppose they talk about you in a certain way or look at you in a certain way. In that case, you will immediately link it to this insecurity you have told them about. When you look at it from the big-picture perspective, this is not a good foundation for getting to know someone as the communication barriers immediately come up.

2. Your past

Many of us are saddled with the burden of our past. This is probably because we have not entirely resolved the issues that we have with it. Therefore, it makes sense that you do not bring this into your new relationship. At some point, the truth is a conversation you are going to have to have with this person. But don't do it at the initial stages when you both are still trying to figure each other out unless of course, you feel that there is some kind of legal implications as a result of their direct connection to you that could impact the nature of the relationship that the both of you are having. Outside of this, give each other a chance to know yourselves in the present. There is going to be plenty of time to discuss your past.

3. Your "truth"

During my awkward social days, I acted like someone who was always on a high dose of the truth serum. Whenever I was in a conversation with anybody new, my lack of confidence and low self-esteem would kick in on high drive, and I would find myself saying things that are true but very disrespectful. I would say this in the most horrible way. I once remember telling my poor date that I thought their outfit was ghastly. Their stunned look of shock is forever engraved in my mind. In retrospect, the outfit was dreadful, but that was not the moment to say it or even how to say it. If I want to give people a chance to know me, I should not make the process difficult. Now, we have already established that communication is complicated. However, an attitude of "telling the truth" when you are basically just making offensive statements can ruin any good opportunity you have before things get off the ground. Keep those comments in your head.

When We Fall for Our Own Lies

One of the things I learned on this journey is that lying is a defense mechanism triggered by a need to protect ourselves and sometimes our loved ones. The occasional fibbing is harmless, but if you don't make a conscious effort to alter the negative words you say to yourself and other people, you will find yourself in a situation where you are falling for your own lies. If this happens, you become disillusioned. A person whose focus on life is not on the realm of reality cannot successfully build a relationship, much less have a meaningful conversation with another person. This is because their mind is always going to be aligned with these falsehoods that they have now adopted as the truth. These statements might seem very foreign to you because the lies that we tell ourselves are not necessarily huge lies. And that is the impressive thing about lying to yourself. One simple statement gradually becomes a daily affirmation, which eventually becomes your reality. You are not even aware of what is happening when it happens.

Lie Number One: Something is Wrong with Us

At the beginning of this book, I did hint that it is human nature to want to communicate or commune with other people, and part of this desire might mean conforming to the general standard. This is why individuality is not always appreciated. This negative way of thinking is something that has been ingrained from our early childhood unless you were lucky enough to have parents who affirmed the positivity that comes with being true to yourself. So, when you find that you are acting different, looking different, or even talking different, you automatically assume that something is wrong with you. This may not be your fault entirely, as society has a way of pointing fingers at us from the moment we come into this world. Perhaps your friends may have told you that you are different, or maybe your parents have drummed it into your head that the desires that you have, your physical, appearance or perhaps the way you act is simply unacceptable. At first, you would fight these words, but over time, your rebellious nature may slow down, and you would begin to take these words that have been spoken to you on repeat as the truth. And so, every time you find yourself acting a little different, rather than address the situation or focus on the problem, you immediately link it to this difference in your nature. I struggled with this for years. I had to understand that being myself is the best gift I could ever give myself, and I want you to take this same message with you. There is absolutely nothing wrong with who you are as long as you are not harming anyone physically, emotionally, and psychologically. As long as you follow the truest path to your heart, you are perfectly normal.

Lie Number Two: You are Not Good Enough

Ask any man or woman who is pining away for the love of their life why they have not made any move or reached out in any way to let this person know that they exist; the answer you would most likely get is that this person is out of their league. Meaning, they feel that they are not good enough. I also was a card-carrying member of this group. I would meet amazing people, and we would have those great instant connections, but for some reason, when I find it going so well, I would immediately recoil into my shell because I feel like I don't deserve that kind of attention or care or whatever it is I was getting at that moment. Mind you, this kind of connection was something I strongly desired. Still, it didn't stop me from folding my hands or throwing it all away. When you feel that you are not good enough, you engage in self-sabotaging behavior. In the area of communication, you start acting strangely or completely cut yourself off from the person. If you go back to past relationships that simply withered away, your narrative before reading this text might be that they left you or they abandoned you. Nonetheless, when you get their own narrative, you would find that there are series of actions or spoken words by you that made them take that decision to walk away. In other words, you played an active role in sabotaging those relationships. Remind yourself every day that you are good enough. The message is not going to sink in overnight. It might take years of affirmation before you start believing it but believe me. When that day comes, the euphoria you feel will make it seem as if you are just reborn. You, my friend, are definitely good enough.

Lie Number Three: You need something to become the person you want to be.

I have heard this lie being told several times. People say if they had that degree or had that relationship or had that car, everything they want in their lives will fall in place. Even communication. But this is not true. Granted, if you look at things in-depth, there might need to be some changes in order to become the person you aspire to be in any given relationship. But those things have little or nothing to do with material things when it comes to character change or personality development. You don't need material objects to become a better version of yourself, or else what you are doing is simply projecting what should naturally come to you on an object. So, when that object is taken away from you, you feel like this personality is also gone. We are more than our jobs, our relationships, or any material possessions we may have. Our need for communication is a response to a basic human need to connect with other people, nothing else. Stop feeding yourself the information that you are not good enough until XYZ happens. That kind of thinking is very self-limiting and needs to stop if you are going to make progress in any relationship. In the next part of this book, you would find that this information I have shared with you here is very relevant to the process ahead of you. Reading people requires a mind that is sound and stable and this whole first part of the book is dedicated to helping you get started with that process. I believe that removing this lie is one of those crucial steps needed for this journey. I want to tell you what a mentor told me. She said, "the only thing that stands between you and your dreams is yourself". Yes, there are going to be many obstacles but none of them can stop you the way you can stop yourself.

Love, Hate, and Everything in Between

Love and hate are powerful emotions that belong on opposite sides of the same coin. This is why the expression "there is a thin line between love and hate is very apt." In this context, I am not talking about romantic relationships. I am actually referring to the relationship that we have with ourselves because, at the heart of every relationship, our perception of the people we engage with is usually a reflection of our own perceptions of ourselves. When you hate yourself, you will most likely perceive hate coming to you from other people. You will find it difficult to trust and rely on anyone not to talk of making an effort to build a healthy relationship with this person.

Whenever we talk about relationships and communication, our immediate focus is on the other person we engage with. We always seem to forget the basic fact that we make up at least half of that relationship, and therefore, we also have a prominent role to play in the direction that communication goes or flows. In essence, I am trying to say that our relationship with other people is basically a reflection of the relationship that we have with ourselves. If you do not have a love for yourself, I can assure you that it would be virtually impossible to have a relationship where love is given and taken in equal measure. Self-love is not just some psychological lingo concocted by peace-loving hippies who live permanently at a meditation camp. It is an expression of how we feel about ourselves, and it is this expression that empowers our ability to interact with other people.

In this chapter, we have talked about the lies that we tell other people, the hard truths that we should keep to ourselves, and the lies we end up falling for. All of this was leading to this point, which is basically an inward look at the image we have of ourselves. I am not talking about what society has been telling you or what your parents have told you. I am talking about what you tell yourself. It doesn't matter if you are struggling with weight loss, financial insecurities, or even a health challenge. Everyone on this planet has a battle that they are fighting, and the one thing that equips you for battle no matter what is self-love. It is the love you have for yourself that will inspire you to get on a treadmill every day even when you feel your back and bones are breaking. It is the love that you have for yourself that will make you step out of your comfort zone to take on new business ventures that will bring you closer to attaining your dreams, and it is the love that you have for yourself that will help you look past the physical limitations we are going to talk about in the next part of this book and take the time to get to know people better. Reading people is an art that is learned, and the first step is learning to read yourself.

Exercise

1. Make an extensive list of things that you feel are stopping you from making progress in any relationship that you have. Don't hold back when you are writing this list. It is important that you delve into your mind's deepest part to reveal what you are really thinking.

2. Go over the contents of this list one item after the other and group them into two categories: others versus you. By others,

I am referring to faults or problems that lie with other people or things. Make sure they are not related to you in any way.

3. When you have successfully separated this list, throw away the list that has to do with others and focus on the one that has to do with you. For the coming hours, days, weeks, or even months, this list is going to be a to-do list. It shows you the steps you must take to resolve those issues until you get to a point where your slate is blank.

4. When you have successfully resolved anything that has to do with you at the helm of affairs, revisit step 1 of this process, write down a list of the things that you feel is standing in your way, and determine what you can do to take care of the problem now.

5. After completing the fourth step take a trip to your journal and write out what you have learned in this process. For example, how do you feel being the one in charge of your own affairs? As for the second list that you threw away, do you have any regrets about it and why?

The exercise goal in this chapter is to help you come to terms with the truth that you are the one in charge of any communication you have with people. Therefore, if there is a problem with the way you communicate or the way you perceive others, or even the way you perceive yourself when you are with other people, there is definitely going to be a problem with communication. The reason for this is that your skewered view of life is going to alter your ability to accurately read and analyze people, much less build a sustainable relationship with them.

Chapter Four

THE COMPLICATED NATURE OF RELATIONSHIPS

Relationships are complicated. This is a fact of life. You want to learn how to read people so that you can do better in the way you communicate? You are going to have to learn to accept this fact and work towards making the most of what you have. Usually, they say before you go on a journey, you must first determine your destination. For us, that is you and I, we want to answer the question of, "what is the point?" In this chapter, we are going to look into what our destination is. For the most part, I would say our destination is a healthy relationship. It doesn't matter whether it is a business relationship or a romantic relationship. At the end of the day, you want it to be healthy. But what does a healthy relationship really mean? How do you identify what is healthy for you? Are there specific markers that you can use, or is this simply one of those elusive things that are only real on social media?

I will try as much as possible to answer those questions in this chapter. However, I want you to pay particular attention to the segment that talks about healthy relationships as well as letting go of toxic relationships. Go into this with an open mind. Remove any preconceived notion you may have. One mistake we often make when it comes to building the foundations for a better working relationship with people is working with assumptions. As we go further on that journey, we then raise our defense mechanisms, especially when confronted with information that does not align with these assumptions. Drop everything that you think you know and open your mind to receive the message that you need in this chapter.

What is a Healthy Relationship?

If you go on the internet and do a little research on healthy relationships, you would find this perfect Hollywood movie type description that would either give you unrealistic expectations or make you very skeptical about attaining such perfection. When you look at these various descriptions and definitions of what a healthy relationship is an objective, they each have their differences and similarities, but the unified message they all give is this; a healthy relationship is the kind of relationship where you and the person you are in that relationship with thrive. Most people look at healthy relationships from a romantic perspective. I am trying to look at it from a broader view. I want to be inclusive, so I try to picture all the types of relationships we have. And so, with that in focus, I would say a healthy relationship is a relationship where the needs of all people involved are effectively communicated, the different views are respected, and the individuals involved have a platform to thrive.

In a business situation, both parties are secure in the dealings they have with each other as there is a high level of trust between the people involved. Here, the rules of engagement have been clearly stated and communicated to the understanding of all the people that are working together on that business project. A healthy business relationship is not just money-centric. It is also rooted in ensuring that the persons involved are taken care of financially, legally, and otherwise. Business relationships where one or both parties have serious doubts about the other's intentions will only lead to chaos, unnecessary drama, and a lot of miscommunication. You will find a lot of underhandedness where one party or both parties are determined to outplay the other person so that they can reap the benefits of the deal that is being worked on together. This situation is mentally unhealthy and can cause the ruin of a person.

A healthy romantic relationship is like a business relationship, except that there is intimacy involved. Both partners can communicate at a frequency that they both understand clearly.

There is trust as well as security in the knowledge that both partners are working with each other's best interest at heart. A healthy romantic relationship reinforces a lot of positivity in the lives of the individuals involved. It does not mean that there is an absence of disagreements or discord. Instead, you would find that even in the midst of a disagreement, communication does not break down or disintegrate to the point where emotional responses turn negative.

The 5 Key Elements of a Healthy Relationship

In the last segment, you wolves notice that there are keywords I used in describing a healthy relationship. In this segment, I will highlight these keywords as they will help you determine the kind of relationship you have currently and give you a mental image of what you should aspire for. If any of these elements are missing in your relationship, you might not be in a good situation.

1. Trust

Any relationship that has Trust absent in it cannot be tangible, sustainable, or healthy. Trust is what holds the fabric of a relationship together, especially when you have to weather the storms that life throws at you. When you trust a person, it means that you can rely on that person, whether it is for advice or aid in the time of help. Trust is not something that is immediately given. Sometimes, you have to build on this over time. The sad thing about trust is that it can easily be broken, and when that happens, it is even more difficult to regain. But if you get to a place where you have firmly established trust and the other person also trusts you in equal measure, you are in a healthy relationship.

2. Security

Nobody wants to be in a relationship with the person who makes them feel as though they cannot go to sleep with both eyes closed. You want to be with someone who has your best interest at heart. A relationship is healthy when both parties involved in that relationship are confident that their mental, physical and emotional health is in no danger or harm from the person with whom they are engaged in a relationship with. In very simple terms, when you are in a healthy relationship, you feel safe and secure. You don't fear that this person is going to cheat you in a business relationship or cheat on you in a romantic relationship. You trust that the secrets you share with them would remain between the people involved.

3. Conflict resolution

Even in perfect relationships, disagreements are bound to happen. The way you resolve those disagreements is an indicator of how healthy your relationship is. If you feel that you have to outshout the other person down or use violent/physical means to get your point across, you may need to re-evaluate the terms of your relationship. In a healthy relationship, the parties involved are able to articulately express themselves without fear or judgment and then reach a compromise even when they are not able to come to the same page in the book. And guess what enables you to make a compromise in such a situation? Trust and security.

4. Individuality

There is a common expression that is used to describe marriage. It says two people become one. In some ways, this is true, but a lot of people misunderstand this to mean that these two different individuals start believing, acting, and thinking like one. There should be a healthy expression of oneself in a healthy relationship without needing to become like the other person. I mean that you can retain your individual personality even though both of you are working together as a team. It is your unified goals and objectives that require both of you to act as one unit. Have your collective goals and values but ensure that you are still focused enough to find room to pursue personal past times.

5. Shared objective

When two people come together, the main thing that keeps them together is a shared objective. As I mentioned earlier, an expression of individuality is a requirement in any healthy relationship. However, no matter how "individual" you are, you still need to have that value or objective that keeps you together. Think of military troops when they are broken into units. Does each member of the team have their own individual personality? Yes. As a matter of fact, is it encouraged? Double yes. But when they go on missions, they are not thinking of themselves individually. They focus on what they are meant to accomplish together so they put in their best form and try to make up for each other's weaknesses. Again, it doesn't matter if it is a business relationship or a romantic relationship; this concept remains the same. For a business relationship, I would imagine making a profit or promoting the company's objective would be the shared objective. In a relationship, it could be marriage or some other form of long-term commitment.

Preparing Yourself Mentally and Emotionally for a Healthy Relationship

By now, I am sure that you can see the common thread. Everything comes back to you. If you want a healthy relationship, you would have to start with the person in the mirror. The reason for this is very simple. If you are not prepared for a healthy relationship, even when you find yourself in one, you will still be dysfunctional and unable to appreciate what you have. As a matter of fact, even when you have the five key elements I have noted in the previous segment, you still may not be able to recognize what a real healthy relationship looks like. There is going to be a lot of work to get you in the right frame of mind for a healthy relationship, but these three tips can help you get started.

1. Accept yourself for who you are

First off, there is no such thing as perfect. Some people may look perfect, but that is only because you are staring at the cover of a book. We all have our internal struggles. It is just that some of us have become very skilled at hiding our flaws. You may not be where you want to be in life, but there is one thing that you are that no one else in the world can be: you are you, flaws, warts, strengths, and all. Accept this fact. I would say you should go as far as embracing your uniqueness.

2. Be open

Life never plays out exactly the way we want it to. No matter how well you plan or how organized you are, there will always be these tiny storms that life throws at you. For people who like to be in control, this might be an earth-shattering truth, but when you are dealing with people outside of yourself, you have to learn to be open. Reading people requires a lot of patience, objectivity, and wisdom. But you need an open mind to truly connect with people.

3. Consider other perspectives

I am a strong advocate for self-care. Stand up for yourself. Always make sure that you take the time to check in with yourself mentally. However, in a relationship, you are going to be involved with other people, and no matter how much you bond over little things that matter to you, like favorite colors, favorite food, or even nationality, there will always be a matter of perspective. The way you see life is going to be different from the way the other person sees life. Disagreement often arises as a result of these differences in perspectives. So, start grooming yourself now to learn how to look at things from other people's points of view even as you stand up for your own rights. I believe it makes it easier for communication and negotiation.

Letting Go of Toxic Relationships

As we wrap up this final chapter in the first part of this book, I am going to close it off with this very important task. Right now, the only person that can determine what your current relationship status is, whether it is business or romantic, is you, so you will have to do some soul searching in that regard. If you are looking for something new and you want to build a foundation for something that is healthy, you would need to let go of the negative relationships in your life. Previously, when I talked about negative lies and misconceptions that we have allowed to become an integral part of our lives, I did say that it is important for you to let go of those thinking patterns. The next step in that process is to let go of people who encourage such thinking patterns.

Unfortunately, some of these relationships are with people you are strongly linked to like parents, siblings, or close friends you have known for years. This makes the thought of letting them go even more painful, especially when you consider the amount of investment to have put into making that relationship work. But I want to remind you that the future you are trying to build for yourself is way more important than what you have in the past. And if what you have right now is not going to help you move forward, what is the point of holding on to it. Remember, in any healthy relationship, you are supposed to thrive, but if you find yourself bending over backward just so you can survive rather than thrive, it becomes imperative that you cut ties with such people and establish new ties.

The idea of starting over with someone can be very scary. Trust me. I know, and this is why this book was created. This first part of the book was to help you understand human behavior and why we do what we do because by understanding this fundamental concept. You will be able to make a more accurate interpretation of the information you are going to get in the next part of the book. Think of this next step as laying the bricks, and I know that you are excited about what comes next. However, to avoid carrying dead weight with you, you need to let go.

Exercise

1. Write down your goals and objectives for your next relationship. What do you hope to happen? I would encourage you to take a moment to paint a vivid picture of what you would like your next relationship to look like. Write this in past tense so that it would be as if you have already experienced it. The purpose of this is to affirm your expectations and dreams.

2. Go over everything you have learned so far from the first chapter to this chapter and note the lessons you have learned, especially the one you feel you connect with the most. Explore the message behind this by doing additional research on the topic. You need to find out why it resonates with you so deeply.

3. Take an objective look at all the relationships that you have. What is your relationship with your biological family like? What about your chosen family? Are things okay? Would you say that your relationship is healthy or toxic? If you had to sieve through those relationships, which would you retain and work on? Which would you let go of? Write your answers down and start taking actionable steps toward your relationship goals.

Part Two:

The Art of Reading

People

Chapter Five

UNDERSTANDING YOURSELF FIRST

O ne of my favorite Pinterest quotes of all time is the phrase, "Physicians know thyself." If you truly want to understand people to improve your communication and socialize better with them, you must factor yourself into the equation. Understand yourself. And that is what this chapter is going to be about. We will be revisiting some of the things we have already talked about in the previous part of the book but with a more defined focus.

Defining Your Goals, Dreams, and Values

When I start to pursue my goals and ambitions in life, I don't start from a place of comfort. Doing the opposite of this is a mistake that a lot of us make. We try to create our goals, dreams, and aspirations from a place that makes us feel secure and comfortable. If you want the kind of results that will truly impact and create the kind of transformation you are looking for in your social life, you have to start with the uncomfortable questions, which is where we have another misunderstanding. There is a general notion that discomfort or questions that are not comfortable are meant to negatively impact your psyche or on your physical circumstance.

On the contrary, an uncomfortable question is a type of question that changes your perspective and forces you to look inward. If it does more than that, you are veering off into another territory. An example of an uncomfortable question when it comes to setting goals is, what would you do if you didn't have to worry about the budget, people's opinions, or failure? Do you see how this question quickly changes the dynamics of your thinking process? This is because then you are no longer thinking of limitations or things that would hold you back. Instead, you are now truly seeing yourself for what you are and seeing the potential of your dreams.

From this point, you can now backpedal and refine those things you usually thought of as your dreams. This process helps you understand yourself a lot better. You are able to come to terms with what your true desires are, and if you pluck up enough courage, you will be able to create a step-by-step process that will help you achieve those dreams. So, let's say you aspire to be a public speaker or to make new friends in your new location. The kind of questions you should be asking is, what would you do if people's opinions were not an issue? As a motivational speaker, author, and as someone who had to undergo that social awkwardness phase, I can tell you that the biggest barrier for socially introverted people who desire to go out more is the fear of what other people will think.

Dump that fear, and you would have mastered the first step in transforming your social life.

Knowing Your Relationship Expectations

Now that you know what you want in yourself, it is time for you to set your expectations for the people in your life. There is a common saying that *if you never want to be disappointed in life, don't have an expectation.* This is so wrong. Not only does it force you to lower your standards in terms of the kind of people you deal with, it actually has the opposite effect because it creates an emotional distance between you and the people you are hoping to connect with. And most importantly, you cannot avoid the disappointments that this kind of mindset comes with because, believe it or not; you attract what you think. So, if you expect the worst in people, chances are most of the people you deal with will be of the worst sort. The best thing to do would be to take a moment and reflect on what you expect out of the relationship that you have with people before taking things a step further.

When defining the qualities that you feel the people in your circle should have, try as much as possible to micromanage every detail of that list. This is because, at the end of the day, the only way you can get everything you want is if you build that person out of clay or metal from scratch. And even then, there is still a chance that the person may not turn out the way you want. The funny thing is that the reason for this inability to function according to your expectation is not really because of the person. It is because of you. As humans, we evolve whether we want to or not, and over time the things that appeal to you today will no longer be appealing tomorrow. Think of that SpongeBob shirt that you thought you could not live without when you were nine years old. Chances are, you haven't seen that shirt in years, and even if you saw it now, you might keep it for sentimental reasons, but you are not going to wear it.

So, how do you set your expectations for people that you are yet to come in contact with?

1. Focus on the quality of character rather than personality

The difference between these two is that one of them lasts for a lifetime while the other depends on their mood. A person might be bubbly and generally cheerful, but you can be sure that a change in their mood will alter their bubbly state. However, when it comes to the quality of a character, choosing a person who has a positive attitude over a bubbly personality will mean that even in dire situations, that person with a positive attitude will be able to sustain that positivity.

2. Reflect on what you want to see

They say that opposites attract. This is very true when it comes to a magnetic field. In real-life scenarios, it is not always the case. If you are a negative person, you will find that you kind of attracts negative people to you. The main reason for that is positive people are also looking for positive influences in their lives. It is possible that they spotted your negativity a mile away and took off in the opposite direction. For this same reason, you can't expect loyal friends if you yourself do not have a single bone of loyalty in your body.

3. Be open-minded

Being open-minded doesn't mean that you open yourself to everything that comes your way. It simply means that you hold off your judgment and character analysis until you have gotten to know a person a little bit better. Sure, the tips you get in this book will help you make some quick assessments of a person's behavior, but if you truly want to build a relationship with that person, you still need to dig a little deeper. I prefer the social cliche, *never judge a book by its cover,* for this kind of situation. I believe that when you meet people, their personality is usually what you see first and remember what I said about personality. It is very fleeting as it depends on the mood. However, the true character of a person lies underneath that crusty exterior.

Setting Boundaries and Defining Your Limits

One of the main reasons you find that people are tolerating the people in their relationships rather than enjoying them is because they failed to set boundaries. And the failure to set boundaries is usually because we have this mindset that boundaries are negative. We feel that people should be able to have access to you no matter what. This "feeling" is further justified if you call these people your friends. Sadly, the advent of social media has gone even further to blur those boundary lines that we are supposed to set. It's like having perfect strangers lounging in your bedroom while you are in your underwear.

Here's a quick fact my mentor threw at me during my early learning stages. She said there are boxes for every person that you meet in life. You have the acquaintance box. You have the spouse box. You have the family box; then you have the friendship box. Even amongst your friends and family, there is a hierarchy in terms of their relevance or importance to you. You have the person that you normally go to for advice. You have the friend that you go-to when it comes to business dealings and transactions. You have the person that you go to when you are feeling vulnerable, and so on. All these different boxes mean there have to be boundaries. The way you treat an acquaintance should not be the way you treat a friend, and the way you treat someone you consider your closest ally and friend should not be the same way you treat someone you just happened to have known for years.

Setting boundaries is for your own peace of mind as well as your mental health. It helps you define how you relate to a person. For me, the important part of setting boundaries is that it helps you define your expectation for that relationship, and hello! That is the purpose of this chapter. Sort the people you meet right off the bat. Decide on where you want to place them, and when you put them in that box, treat them accordingly. It doesn't have to be in a demeaning way. Just because one person is an acquaintance, and the other person is your friend doesn't mean that they are less human. It just means the way you communicate with them is going to be different. Also, your expectations from them will be different.

Doing an Emotional Health Assessment

Being in the right state of mind is a prerequisite for any relationship that you get into. If you are toxic, negative, and filled with all this emotional drama, rather than seeking out new relationships, it is time to take a step back and start building a relationship with yourself. People are shy for many reasons, but if you ask around, you will find that top of that list would be a lack of confidence in themselves and low self-esteem.

You have to admit to yourself that no level of social connection is going to fix what is internally broken right now. You also need to know that being broken does not mean that you are doomed. Everybody at some point in their life became broken in a specific area. Yours just happen to be in the area of being social. Admitting this problem is a crucial step to fixing it.

After listing out all the things that you want in people, take a moment to list out what you want in yourself. Do you feel you are not so articulate? Think about the things that you can do to help you speak better. Do you feel that your fashion sense is way off the beaten track? Figure out the things that you can do to make you blend in a while retaining your identity. In other words, look at the things that you can fix now and start working on them. Enjoy a beautiful relationship with yourself. When this happens, you will find it easier to attract and connect with people who also find you appealing.

Exercises

As per usual, whip out your journal and take quick notes on the following things –

1. Describe yourself in three words

2. List out the things that you like about yourself

3. Write down three qualities you wish you had as a person

Next, make a list of 3 people who you trust the most and feel will be able to give you honest answers. They don't have to be your friends or family members, and if you feel like this might be too awkward, just tell them that you are trying to do a survey for some company and you need their help to create a character profile. Now ask these questions and take note of their responses

1. Ask them to describe you in three words. They don't need to explain those words. Let them just say it as it comes to their head.

2. What are the things you do that they like and appreciate? You may not get much of a response from acquaintances but still, encourage them to answer by telling them that it doesn't matter how little or insignificant it is. You just want to get their perception of you.

3. Is there anything they wish you did more often? This usually hints at things that people feel you are capable of. It is meant to basically highlight your potential from the perspective of other people. When you are done compiling information from these three people, compare it to what you wrote down initially about yourself. Are there any similarities? If there are, put that aside now. If there aren't, look at those things, they say they like and appreciate you. Are those qualities you would like to build on? Do you think those qualities can improve communication in relationships? If so, start working on a plan to build on those qualities. Now go back to that list of similarities. Categorize them as either negative or positive. If they are negative, start working on a plan to eliminate that character trait. If they are positive, start thinking of the things you can do to build on this.

Chapter Six:

BODY LANGUAGE

When it comes to reading people, we focus so much on what people say when in reality, it is the nonverbal cues that pack the most information. Communication experts will tell you to read between the lines, but if you really want to figure someone out, it is not the lines they are speaking about that you should be reading. The real scoop lies in what their eyes are saying, the way they move certain parts of their body when they make certain sentences, and even those weird ticks could be a clue. The art of reading body language is something that intelligence agencies have utilized to their advantage for years. Body language is an open secret, the hidden message that is right under your nose, and in this chapter, we are going to dissect it and help you figure out what it's about.

The Science Behind Body Language

Before we delve into this topic properly, here is a fun fact. There is actual science that is focused on the study of body language. It is called kinesics. This study involves the interpretation of nonverbal cues and has played a very important role in uncovering those hidden communication skills we were absolutely clueless about. Now that we have gotten the academic stuff out of the way let us bring this back to our day-to-day living. According to experts, 60% to 65% of our daily communication is in our body language. This is huge! What it means is that the bulk of what you say is not actually said in your words. Your mouth may do some talking, but it is your body that does most of the communicating.

Interestingly, you would think that having different cultural backgrounds, religious upbringing, race, ethnicity, social status, and so on would mean we have to learn those nonverbal cues in different languages as well. I mean, think about it. There are over 6000 spoken languages. Would it be the French nonverbal equivalent of a noncommittal shrug? But the experts tell us that body language is actually a universal language. So, the expressions that we are going to talk about in this chapter are valid wherever you go. There may be slight differences in how these signals are interpreted, but fundamentally, our bodies speak the same language wherever we are.

How to Interpret Facial Expressions

As I mentioned earlier, our body language transcends geographical locations and language barriers. According to research, seven universal facial expressions cut across the board, and these expressions are pretty much the same. So even if you don't understand a word of what the person is saying, the expression on their faces tells you exactly what they are currently feeling. Now, remember, knowing the emotion a person is experiencing is one thing. Identifying the cause of that emotion is something different entirely. There are several micro facial expressions besides the universal facial expressions. We will get into that later.

The universal facial expressions are listed as;

1. Surprise

This is the feeling you experience when you encounter something or a completely unexpected situation. Some psychologists and sociological experts do not consider surprise to be emotion because it is neither negative nor positive, and they feel that for anything to be considered an emotion, it has to be one of either. Whatever the case, the surprise could be triggered by positive or negative experiences. However, do not confuse surprise with being startled. The most common facial expression associated with surprise is the jaw drop. Then you have the raised eyebrows, which are not joined together, and finally the eyes. The upper eyelid is raised in tandem with the eyebrows, while the lower eyelid remains neutral.

2. Fear

Fear is what you experience when you feel impending danger or harm coming your way either physically, psychologically, or emotionally. When you experience fear in excess, it becomes paranoia. But the absence of fear can lead you to make risky decisions that could negatively impact your life. Having this in mind, we can determine that fear is an emotion born out of self-preservation. Sometimes, it is easy to confuse fear with surprise. This usually happens when the emotion that follows surprise is fear, but they are clear expressions that tell you what is being experienced. You should also bear in mind that there are different stages of fear. You have that initial stage of trepidation before getting to the height, which is terror. There is also the jaw drop in the facial expression of fear, but the lips are drawn backward in this instanced. As with surprise, the eyebrows are also lifted, but they are drawn together in this case. You would find that the upper eyelid is raised around the eyes while the lower eyelid is tensed.

3. Disgust

No one can see a rotten egg put on their plate without having a negative reaction to what they smell and see. I am pretty sure it will not even get to the point of touching, much less touching it because of the level of disgust you would experience. Disgust is an emotion that arises as a result of your aversion to something. From my example, you can determine that it is triggered by what you experience with your five physical senses. When a person is truly disgusted, you get verbal cues from the person through words like "yuck" or "ew." There are also instances where the person begins to gag. The most common facial expression of disgust is the wrinkling of the nose. The eyebrows become lowered; the upper lip becomes an inverted 'U' with the lower lip puckering out just a little bit. Some people use their hands to supplement the emotion by covering their mouth or nose. This happens especially when the level of disgust is high.

4. Contempt

When you experience contempt for a person, basically, you are engaging in the feeling that you are superior to a person. To be more specific, you feel that these emotions are directed towards being lesser than you. Contempt is not full-on hate as that is more intense. Instead, you find it more common in situations where people of lower status feel content for the people who are socially superior to them even though they feel the reverse is the case in their minds. There have been cases where people in higher positions of power feel contempt towards people in lower positions. This usually happens when they feel that this person does not deserve whatever good may have come that way. Contempt in facial expression is visible when one side of the corner of a closed mouth is tightened and raised.

5. Anger

Anger is what you experience when you feel that you are wronged or have suffered some form of injustice. It also happens when you get the sense that your rights have been trampled on or you are being treated in a manner that you consider poor. Physical and emotional hurt is also known to trigger anger. There are a few ranges of emotions that fall within the range of anger. From mild annoyance to complete rage, there are other emotions in between that connotes anger. Facial clues of a person's anger are the eyebrows drawn together, the eyes staring wide and hard, and then the lips tightly closed.

6. Sadness

Sadness is one of those emotions that has a range of feelings on the emotional spectrum. Typically, we experience sadness when there has been a loss. It doesn't have to be the loss of a person alone. As long as something of value is no longer present in your life, you will experience this emotion. People often assume that sadness is automatically negative. This is not always the case, especially if you look at it from the perspective of how it serves you. Sadness is just a sign that you are in need of comfort. You can see the sadness in a person's facial expression when the eyebrows' inner corners are pulled up. As for the eyes, the upper eyelids become droopy while the eyes themselves look downward. Depending on the degree of sadness experienced, the person's mouth's outer corners will be pulled downwards.

7. Happiness

If you prefer, happiness or enjoyment is one emotion that we all want to experience as often as possible. A lot of us go through some of the things that we do in our lives because the objective is to reach the place of complete happiness. Happiness has a way of genuinely energizing you, and it keeps you in a positive state of mind. This is a stark contrast to sadness, which drains you completely and gives you a dark view of the world. Interestingly, people might use their verbal cues as well as other biological resources to try and fool you into thinking they are genuinely happy. However, your facial expression has something else to say no matter how well you try to mask things. The face of a person who is genuinely happy has eyes that are wrinkling at the corners and narrowed. The cheeks are raised while the lips are pulled back to reveal their teeth when they smile.

Body Fluid Secretions and the Hidden Messages

As unpleasant as this sounds, there are certain emotions you will experience that would automatically trigger the secretion of body fluids. I remember back in my heyday when my social anxiety was in overdrive. I used to sweat a lot whenever I was presented with the opportunity to speak with another person. I just could not handle it. My palms will become sweaty. My forehead would be sweaty, and even my armpits will be sweating up a storm. From experience, I can tell you that anxiety sweat smells different and not in a good way.

Suppose you take a walk down memory lane. In that case, there is a strong possibility that you may have also heard this embarrassing nervous sweat situation happen to you, and this is your moment to turn that information into something that will pay out in your relationships later. When you watch people interact, no matter how confident they feel on the exterior, the secretion of body fluids tells you the actual state of their mind. These body fluids could be anything from tears, saliva to sweat. For example, when a person is lying, and you turn up the heat in order to fish out the truth, one involuntary telltale sign that they are lying is sweat on their upper lips. The more elaborate the lie is, the more intense the sweating will be. In fact, you will find the sweat dripping down the sides of their hair.

Tears are also another indication of a person's emotional state of mind. When we see tears, we immediately assume something has happened. But tears are also present when you are emotionally overwhelmed or feeling extremely happy. Now, since our focus is on reading people, we are going to look at one particular type of body fluid and what it means. That body fluid is sweat. When a person sweats in their palms, it's an indication of anxiety and nervousness. When they sweat on the upper lip or forehead as they speak to you, it could be that they are having an internal conflict with the information that they have just shared with you. Of course, you would have to watch out for all the telltale signs that match up to this diagnosis to accurately determine a person's thoughts and implied intentions.

Using Body Posture to Determine People's Perception of You

True story; it is actually possible for a person to stand in front of you, smile at you, and even say some of the nicest things to you but remain completely closed off to you. I have been in that situation more times than I care to count. In this scenario, the fun fact is that they are actually telling you that they are not as into you as their words say. The problem is that you are not reading the signals that they are giving you correctly. So, in this segment, we are going to examine some of those body postures in communication and what it says. This way, you can filter through the niceties and fake smiles and get right to the true nature of their feelings towards you.

1. The locking of arms and other body parts:

When a person's arms or legs are crossed as they face you, it is a clear indication that they have created a space and marked it as their own. They do not want anyone violating that space that they have created. This does not mean that they will not engage in a conversation with you. What they are saying non-verbally is that there are boundaries, and you have to respect that. So, if you intended to come any closer, you might need to stand down if you want to continue communication with this person. The crossing of arms is as good as the person saying, do not come any closer.

2. Mirroring Your Actions:

In situations of a more amorous nature, a clear indication that the person you are talking to is interested in you is a form of posturing called mirroring. In essence, this person will be mirroring certain things that you do. This act is not entirely conscious, but it speaks volumes when it comes to how they really feel about you. For instance, if you sit down and place one elbow on the bar counter and the person opposite you does the same, that person is interested in you. Unlike the previous posture, this one is saying that you should continue the conversation in a direction that probably will lead to more intimacy.

Exercise

The purpose of the exercise in this chapter is to help you build confidence. Whether you are getting on stage to talk to a group of people or planning to insert yourself into more social situations, this guide will help you project confidence even when you feel like running into your room, locking the doors, and staying hidden.

1. Practice your handshake

A firm grip tells people that you are capable and reliable. Tell yourself this every time someone reaches out that hand to shake it. Make it a part of your routine. Keep it firm but not too tight. Always remember this.

2. Maintain eye contact

During my socially awkward years, I noticed that I found it extremely difficult to look at anyone in the eye. The moment I made eye contact; I could feel myself dissolving from the inside. Start practicing this before you get into an actual social situation. When next you are at the bus stop, focus on one random stranger. If they look at you, nod your head and smile, and whatever you do, don't immediately turn your gaze away.

3. Stop fidgeting

Fidgeting with your clothes when you are in a social situation tells your audience that you are not comfortable or confident in what you are wearing at least. So, before you even step into such situations, make sure you get the right fit of clothes and wear a style that is both comfortable and suitable for the occasion. For those of us that like to bite our nails, I find that keeping our hands preoccupied with something helps reduce your tendency to do this.

Chapter Seven

DECIPHERING VERBAL CUES

Most of the content of this book is focused on the hidden language that people use to communicate, which is basically the expressions and their faces as well as the way they position their bodies. However, I want you to also remember that according to the statistics I gave earlier on, 60%-65% of communication is done through body language. This means that 35% to 40% is done verbally. The key to deciphering what people are saying is to actually listen and pay attention to what is being said and not just that. In this chapter, you are going to learn how to decode and read people by listening to how they speak.

Reading Between the Lines

If it seems like you are the only one struggling with communication in any situation, you are wrong. It is not always easy for us to express what we truly feel. This is why subconsciously, our body does this for us. At the end of the day, we really want other people to know how we are feeling. Now the next step in that process is for people to understand the signs you are giving, which is why this book was written; to empower you and enable you to decipher people's thoughts. In verbal communication, words are not just what is being said. It also has a lot to do with what is being implied. This is where reading between the lines comes in. You have to be able to distinctively understand the message that is being passed across to you.

Sometimes, those words are not expressively spelled out. You would have to do a little bit of mathematics in that you add one here and another there and then make sense of what the person is really saying. Let me illustrate what I mean. I met my ex on a dating platform. But before I went to this platform, I went through all of these dating classes and read a lot of books on the subjects to help me become more adept at communication. It paid off beautifully because when we first started talking, we hit things off right away. The conversation was slick and smooth, and as a man, I had to remind myself that it was important for me to take things at her own pace. However, at some point in our conversation, she said something in the lines of, *I cannot wait to hear the sound of your voice.*

I literally took those words and figured she meant she was okay with our conversation and was looking forward to when we would start talking over the phone. Three days later, when I finally asked for her phone number, she laughed and then asked me why it took me that long to do this. I told her that I was just going with the flow of a conversation, and she said she had already indicated she wanted to have my phone number. Mortified, I frantically searched through our conversation, thinking I had missed something. It was then I went back to these exact words that she had written. She said she could not wait to hear the sound of my voice. This implied she was ready for a phone conversation, but that meaning completely flew over my head because I was waiting for her to explicitly ask for my phone number. During a conversation with people in our day-to-day lives, things like this happen. So, you had to learn to pay attention to what is being said. But as I mentioned earlier, it doesn't end there. You have to understand how it is being said, and for that, we are moving to the next segment.

Using the Tone of the Voice to Determine Emotional State

Voice inflections indicate the amount of emotional stress we are undergoing. High pitched sounds tend to connote fear, anxiety, and concern, while low pitched sounds could be an indication of sadness or, in some cases, anger. It may not be easy to immediately detect emotions in the sounds of people's voices as that may require you to get to know them a little bit more. But there are things that can help you read people's emotions. You also have to remember to put the events surrounding that conversation into consideration before coming to a conclusion.

1. Breathlessness

When there is a level of breathlessness in a person's voice, it could mean one of three things. They are either nervous about this communication with you or have some emotional attraction towards you and are trying their best to hide it. Thirdly, it is also possible that they are having difficulty breathing as they talk. This could indicate some kind of health problems that cause breathlessness or that they engaged in some kind of physical activity right before they started talking with you. Use the context of your conversation to decode what this breathlessness means.

2. Speed

When people are nervous or anxious, they tend to talk faster. This is why people with speech impairment stutter when they are emotionally agitated. There is so much they are trying to figure out in their mind that the words just pour out without much thought to it. On the opposite end of the spectrum, when a person slows their speech down and pairs it with a lot of conversation fillers like um, ah, it could mean that they are trying to think as they speak, which in some cases tells you that they are lying.

3. Deliberate Pauses

When a person talks and takes deliberate pauses during their conversation, they are trying to emphasize the message that is being communicated to you. This is an indication that what is being said is very important, so you better pay attention to it. The pauses allow them to create emphasis on meaningful words so that you have the chance to grasp the implied or direct meaning.

The Face Value of Spoken Words

When it comes to socializing and communication, humans can be both complex and simple at the same time. This is one of the most intriguing things I have discovered on my journey to learn how to read and understand people better. As much as we like to look for hidden clues in conversations to help us understand people better, we cannot ignore the fact that sometimes the things that people say are simple and direct, with no need for clues to help you decipher what is spoken.

Some people have that direct way of communication that can be both puzzling and refreshing. When you meet a person like this, it is safe to say that you can take everything they say at face value. Of course, their body language and facial expressions as well as other forms of non-verbal communication, will hold more clues as to what they are really thinking and feeling. But at the end of the day, you can rely on the words that are being said because they mean it. Such people do not engage in theatrics, nor do they use long and elaborate speeches to lay out the message in their hearts.

Communication with people who like to be direct is usually short and straight to the point. They do not beat about the bush. Sometimes, they may be hesitant about telling you what they want, but if you understand that this is how they communicate, mirroring the same communication tactics will help you make the most of that relationship. So, ask your questions directly. This way, you will receive direct answers, and everyone goes home happy.

Speech Patterns and their Role in Communication

All speech patterns basically refer to how we talk, and sometimes, the environment that we are in can influence our speech patterns. For instance, the way you speak with your colleagues at work would be different from the way you speak with your childhood friends who have known you since forever. Your voice also houses your personality. There are certain phrases and colloquialisms you use when talking that can show where you are from, how you are feeling, and sometimes what your intentions are.

When you are trying to read people, pay attention to these details because these speech patterns can give you clues that will help you get to know a person better. For example, a person might try to pull off a British accent when in fact; they are from New Orleans. No matter how well their acting is, there are certain colloquialisms used by people from New Orleans that you don't find in British conversations that tell you either this person has some connection to the city or the British accent might not be as authentic as they are trying to make it look.

Other things to look out for in people speech pattern that will help you with them better are;

Rhythm

People who have that flat, monotonous rhythm basically are people who do not like engaging in conversations with crowds. Even when they speak in front of a group, it is possible that this has more to do with the nature of their job than their personality. Those who are able to inject rhythm and personality into the voice are more professional speakers or, at the very least, very comfortable talking to people.

Clarity and Eloquence

Barring any speech impairments, clarity in the way a person speaks can indicate their level of education. A person who has attained a university degree will be more eloquent in the speech pattern than a person who dropped out of high school. It could also be an indication of their social pedigree. People who were brought up in wealth and affluence have a different way of speaking when you compare it with people who have been used to the absence of wealth all their lives.

Exercise

Even with the best manuals on how to read people, your ability to do this successfully is dependent on your knowledge of social and cultural issues. So, it is important that you pack in as much information as possible about people, places, culture, and even religion.

The exercise in this chapter is very straight forward. Take your time and read up on geographical locations that are close to you. Write out a list of biases you have about these places or religions, and then do additional research on the subject. The information that you uncover will be surprising and very helpful.

The best profilers in intelligence agencies are well-read on the subject of culture, geography among other things. Suppose you want to be able to understand people better. In that case, you need to make a habit of reading about people and places if you get the chance to watch movies and documentaries that will help expand the knowledge you already have, take it. This exercise is not a one-time thing. It is something that you should be doing consistently over time.

Chapter Eight

PERCEPTION VS. INTERPRETATION

If you are going to read people, one important skill you must learn and master is to accurately detach your emotions from the situation. The way you feel can cloud your judgment, and this will, in turn, impact the feedback that you are getting from people. In this chapter, the objective is to help you learn how to separate your feelings and opinions from this process of reading people so that the message you get is the real deal.

How to Tell if You are Projecting Your Own Emotions

There are instances when the way you feel about a situation influences your ability to objectively make an analysis. Let's say, for example, you meet this girl of your dreams, and you are so desperate to be with her that even the way she says hello breathlessly might be interpreted to mean that she has some kind of attraction to you because you have read here that breathlessness means interest. However, you cannot rely on that interpretation 100% because your own emotions are involved in the situation. So, how do you tell if you are emotionally interpreting the signals?

1. Your expectations weigh in heavily

What you hope to get out of that relationship can alter the interpretation of the signals that you receive. So, if your expectations for that relationship is very high, chances are you are already emotionally invested. In my opinion, when this happens, you are too emotionally attached to make any accurate assessment

2. You are making up too many excuses

Suppose you find yourself in a situation where you are trying to justify or explain away certain behaviors or things you interpret as negative. In that case, it is possible that you are already emotionally invested, and this might interfere with your ability to properly analyze the signals that you are reading.

3. You are firmly rejecting any narrative that doesn't match your expectation

This is often the case when the feedback you are getting is negative. Rather than face the reality of the situation, you choose to be in denial. This also happens in reverse too. Like a situation where you are expecting people to fall short of your standards so much that even when you see positive signs, you reject them and focus on the negatives you have projected. The fact is, the signs are there in your face. All you have to do is find the courage to accept the truth and work things out from there.

Letting Your Instincts Lead

Detaching yourself emotionally when you are trying to read people doesn't mean that you cannot have an opinion about the person when you are reading people. Experts will tell you that one of the main ingredients in this process is your gut feeling. That moment of connection is often inspired by something some people choose to call premonition or instinct. This is why the saying; first impressions last forever is very popular.

When you meet a person, you lay a psychological imprint on that person. Not because of your actions, words, or charming personality. It has more to do with their natural biological instincts. People who are very entuned with their instincts will align their next course of action with this thought process. From my personal experience, working with your instincts when it comes to socializing with people helps you simplify the process because you can intuitively know what area to concentrate your questions on.

This especially true if you are considering taking that relationship beyond the first meeting. The information you get from this book alone is enough to make you feel a little confused every time you meet a new person because you are not sure where to start your analysis. But if you allow your instincts to guide you, you will intuitively listen to specific words, watch out for their body language, or concentrate on facial expression. This is what I mean by allowing your Instincts to simplify the process.

Making a Factual Assessment of Your Reaction to People

This segment is about helping you ensure that you keep things 100% real with yourself. I made a list that can act as a guide. Follow through on this, and you cannot go wrong.

1. Let go of assumptions

Whatever it is you think you know about people based on a preconceived notion that you have can never go well in any personality assessment. Toss whatever you think you know out of the window and give yourself (and the person in question) a chance to get to know each other before coming to a decisive conclusion.

2. Stop being judgmental

A person's outward appearance does not always reflect what you see on the inside. I am sure that you have heard the saying, "looks can be very deceptive." If you meet a person and you find that you are making your assessment of them based on their outfits, the kind of phone they carry, or some other superficial stuff, you might be blocking out your ability to accurately read the signals that matter. Even if the conversation you are having with them is to determine their financial status, they are other things besides their clothing choice.

3. Looking for something specific

My grandmother told me that if you go looking for something, you will probably find it. I have been looking for a million dollars, by the way, and I'm still hoping to find it. But that is beside the point. When it comes to dealing with people, you cannot start the process of reading them by having a preconceived notion about them. You need to go at it like an open book. Set aside your opinions and thoughts and just work with the information they give you verbally and nonverbally. Going with an open mind will allow you to tune into your instincts even better.

First Impressions and their Lasting Implications

To wrap up this chapter, you should pay attention to something very important, especially when you are meeting people for the first time. The energy that you give off to people will be mirrored to you. So, more often than not, when you get to experience people for the first time, that impression you have of them may not always be all about them. There is a chance that they were simply giving you the same vibe that you were given them

That is not to say if a person treats you in a terrible way, it means they were getting the vibes from you. Some people are just naturally horrible. But when it comes to relating with people, you have to understand that it is like the tide's push and pull. You get what you give, and so if you want a more relaxed atmosphere where people can feel free to be themselves, you have to work on creating that for them.

This means also working on those subtle facial expressions that could give the vibe that you are judgmental or not open to their personalities or whatever. If you go on the internet and read up on the subject of learning how to read people, it almost sounds as if it is a passive activity, but in reality, you are actively engaged in the process. So, have this in mind when next you get into conversations with people. Remember what I have been saying from the beginning; you are half of any relationship that you have.

Exercises

For this part, we are going to bring the focus back to you. This is to help you become more aware of how you act when you are in public. What social cues are you giving? Do you present yourself as open or closed to a conversation? This section will help you answer those questions and also create a plan that would bring about the changes you want to see in your social life.

1. Attempt to strike a conversation with a total stranger at your favorite bar

Ask them a few questions. Put up your best behavior and see how long that conversation lasts. Then after you have spoken with them and called it a day, write a journal about your experience. Don't focus on how the person who reacted or whatever social cues were able to pick up from them. Instead, talk about the way you were feeling. We will get back to this in a moment.

2. Try having this conversation in a completely different social setting that you are unfamiliar with. As with your last chat with a stranger, take note of your experience. How did it make you feel? What did you most enjoy? Were there any negatives or positives? How long did this conversation last?

If you make a comparison with the last two conversations, you will find that you felt more comfortable in the first place because it was a familiar setting. This helped you to project confidence better and engage more in that conversation, while the second place may have had you focusing more on little details like your appearance and so on

In a situation where you were more comfortable and relaxed, you were able to enjoy that conversation more, but the opposite was the case in that unfamiliar environment. So, you see that your social experience had little or nothing to do with the person you were having a conversation with. The point of this test is to prove that you actually play an active role when it comes to your experiences in conversations with people.

So, before you put yourself in the situation where you are trying to read a person's expression and emotion, make sure that internally you are in a place where you feel confident and relaxed. This way, you can give off the kind of energy that makes people open up better to you. When people feel comfortable in your company, they are more likely going to leave themselves open to read.

 **Part 3:**

Communication and Social Interaction

Chapter Nine

USE OF SPACE IN COMMUNICATION

In the last part of this book, we touched a little bit on how people use their space. I didn't go into details there because I wanted to focus on body language and not talk about the environment and how we interact with our environment. In this chapter, that is going to be our entire focus. The space you find yourself in can influence how you interact or engage with people that come into that space because of this fact. When you are trying to read people, you are going to learn the hard and important rule about reading a room.

How People Interact with Their Environment

Before we start talking about people, we are going to focus on you. You will be the social experiment used to illustrate the point being made in this segment. So, remember the last exercise where you interacted with a complete stranger in an environment where you were completely comfortable with and then try to do the same thing in a new environment? Did you notice how you felt and how those feelings impacted your conversation? Hold on to your heart because everything you learned in that social experiment is going to be unveiled and used here.

The outcome of that experiment is exactly how it plays out when people interact with each other. In an environment where you feel that you are in a safe space, you get this quiet assurance that feeds your confidence. This, in turn, impacts the quality of your conversation because you are no longer self-conscious about little details like your appearance. That is not to say you are not worried about how you look, but you feel more accepted by your environment, and so your attention to that detail is less than if you were in a completely strange place.

They are places that you get to that immediately gives you this sober atmosphere. For example, suppose you walk into a funeral home. In that case, even when there is no active funeral in service, you immediately feel this cold that makes it difficult to engage in positive emotions like happiness, joy, and laughter. Instead, you find that you are more reflective and sober. There is a lot of scientific research to support this. However, this book is more focused on the practical side of things.

That said, when you go to an event, it is important that you try to get a grasp of what the event is about. This will help you determine the mood in the room. When you have been able to accurately determine the mood in the room, this, in turn, will affect or influence the way you communicate with people. As I mentioned earlier, your engagement level will be mirrored back at you. So, if you are able to read the room correctly, there is a higher chance of you getting more positive feedback from the people you are trying to interact with. It is why I included this bit in this book. Reading people is not just in their expression, it is also in the atmosphere that they find themselves in.

The Invisible Lines that Should not be Crossed

In every relationship stare physical and mental boundaries that should be respected if that relationship is expected to progress beyond a certain level out. This book is about getting impressions of people through their body expressions and because we have established that the environment the people find themselves in could influence the way we interact with you I feel that it is necessary to point out some of these boundaries that must be respected

1. Physical space

Physical space is not limited to the home or office area that has been physically assigned to the person in question. As humans, we are naturally territorial. So, wherever we find ourselves in, we sort of carve out a space for us no matter how tiny it is. When you are interacting with someone, if a person steps beyond a certain point, you might feel like your space is being invaded. In an intimate setting, if you're closer than three feet to a person, especially if the person is a stranger, you might be violating their space, and this may cause them to be hostile towards you. Unless you want a hostile response, I would say respect this boundary.

2. Time-space

Without realizing it, we all have our own timings, and this is because of the individual routines as well as the templates that our experiences had given to us. So, when it comes to communication, if you want to get the best result, it is important to pay attention to timing. What do I mean by this? When you meet a person for the first time and take their phone number, you don't immediately call unless, of course, the person giving you some social cues that indicated this. You need to give them some space to process the experience they had with you before reintroducing yourself over the phone. For most people, 24 hours after the first meeting is fantastic. For some other people, you might need to wait at least two days. It may sound like petty games, but this is a very important boundary to respect.

3. Emotional Space

Some people are emotionally unavailable. Not because they want to be jerks or terrible people but because they have some personal stuff they are dealing with. When you read a person during this period, you are going to get a lot of cues that indicate their current emotional state. Now, some of us have a natural tendency to nurture people, and because of this, when you see this many emotional cues, you instinctively want to take the person under your wing and nurture them into a sound emotional state. This is wrong. People like this might need the occasional company every now and then, but at the end of the day, they need that emotional space to help them come to terms with what they are dealing with in a healthy way and then move on before they are ready to deal with new relationships. Your ability to read facial expressions and other forms of non-verbal communication does not give you the right to invade a person's emotional space. Respect this boundary, and you will have laid the ground for a healthy relationship in the future.

Body Language and Space Management

Now that we have fully established the fact that space is very important in the way people engage and interact with each other, the next step is to understand those cues that speak to the possibility that you are doing too much. People are naturally polite and may not want to outrightly tell you that you are invasive, but you can tell exactly how far you have gone through these nonverbal clues. It doesn't matter if the interaction is happening over the phone or in real life. I have you covered.

Real-time conversations

1. Crossed or folded body parts

I talked about this earlier. When a person folds their arms across their chests, what they are saying is stay away from me. If you want to keep engaging in a conversation with that person, take us a step back literally and watch how they respond. If the arms are still folded, and you still see the other signs, you might need to take another step back or quit the conversation entirely.

2. Body parts are away from you

When a person is giving you that side view of their body, it indicates that you are not wanted in their space and are trying to create something else for themselves. This gives the meaning that you either need to step back or that they are not interested in you at all. If their toes are pointing away from you or if their face and eyes are looking at other parts of the room except for you, you might be in their territory, and they do not like it.

3. No eye contact

The absence of eye contact is usually used to indicate that a person is shy. But when you are trying to have a conversation with a person and avoid eye contact, it means they do not want to establish a connection with you. When two people's eyes meet, there is an instant magnetic pull that draws them together. It doesn't matter what your gender is or the purpose of the conversation; you are just drawn to each other. You have the option of either continuing the conversation or taking things somewhere else. But when a person deliberately avoids eye contact with you, it means that you are not wanted where you are right now. Take that as a cue and fall back.

Virtual Communication

1. Monotonous voice pitch

A voice conversation without any emotion is a clear indication that that person does not want to talk to you. Now, there are people who naturally have this monotonic way of speaking. But even then, you would notice these high and low pitches, which indicate emotions. But when there is a complete absence of this, like a bland and a conversation where everything else sounds the same, it is a clue that your call in that particular moment is not appreciated. This doesn't mean you should never call the person again. It just means your timing was off. So, what you should do is to keep that call extra short, extra simple, and perhaps move the conversation to a better time.

2. Long extended pauses

Unless you are in a conversation with a person with whom you enjoy long silences, this is another indication that your timing was wrong and that call should happen later. People who want to be in the conversation actually talk when there are too many long pauses within the space of a short time. It indicates that some emotional barriers prevent that person from talking, or the timing is just not right.

3. Short and Curt Responses

When a person is interested in talking with you, even questions that require a simple yes-or-no answer tend to be longer than two to three sentences. However, if the person is unwilling to talk to you for whatever reason, you will find that their responses are short. For example, you might ask them, *"how did your day go?"*, instead of giving you a detailed outline or a short version of how their day went, you might get something like, *"it was fine,"* and that would be it. Pay attention to this and save yourself the heartache of putting yourself in a situation that makes you feel like you are forcing yourself on people.

Using Non-verbal Cues to Create a Safe Space

With everything that we now know, how can you work on creating a safe space that will provide you with the comfort you need to feel confident and, at the same time, make the person you are communicating with feel comfortable? We are going to answer that question in this segment.

1. Give the right facial expressions

Smile genuinely, look them in the eye and ensure that you are not passive-aggressively giving them cues that will make them feel uncomfortable, like making prolonged eye contact. Timing is essential for this.

2. Add emotion to your voice

Nothing is freakier than spending time in the company of someone who has this single straight tone to the sound of their voice. It is different if you are sitting down in front of a lecture. You have to pay attention to that voice in that scenario. But in a social setting, there are supposed to be more human does voice inflections have a way of soothing a person.

3. Be open

If you want to be able to read people for social reasons, you have to also be open to people reading you. Give out the right kind of vibe so that people will feel comfortable around you. For example, we talked about how crossing your arms is a way of saying, *"don't come any closer."* When you are having a conversation with someone in a social setting, and you do this exact thing, your message is conflicting with what you hope to achieve. Change this, and you will find that people will warm up towards you.

Exercise

One mistake many of us make when it comes to training ourselves to socialize better and understand people in a way that improves communication is that we wait for the opportunity to come rather than create that opportunity ourselves. To change this narrative, I am going to ask you to take a bold step and host someone or some people in your personal space. This can be very scary, especially when you consider the situation going on globally. But there are creative ways to go about this without sacrificing your safety or comfort. For example, you could host your first zoom party.

My first trip to ensuring this party's success is to ensure that you do not overthink the situation. Simply send an invite and then prepare yourself for that conversation. I like to arm myself with a lot of information, starting with what is going on in the world and then building it from there.

My second tip to you would be to avoid a situation where you are mostly doing the talking. A good conversation requires both parties to talk. If you are more than two in this zoom party, try to ensure that everyone has an opportunity to speak by asking thoughtful and considerate questions.

My third tip is to avoid conversations that are steeped heavily in negativity. You do not want to bring down the energy in the room with negative vibes. Focusing on stories that are heart-wrenching can easily do this. Instead, look for positive topics that have a way of energizing you and making you feel warm at the same time. You will also benefit from this.

Chapter Ten

EMOTIONAL INTELLIGENCE

On my journey to transforming my social life and building people skills, I discovered one of many truths. Being emotionally intelligent is key in this process. You have to be able to empathize and connect with people emotionally in order to do an effective job of understanding them. It is a clear case of putting yourself in the other person's shoes. A lot of times, we read people from the outsider perspective, and this will give you the raw data you need to analyze the person but in order to get underneath their skin. You have to be able to analyze the situation from their own perspective, and that is what this chapter is about.

5 Emotions You Should be Able to Detect at a Glance

1. Grief

Grief is typically experienced when someone has gone through some kind of loss. When a person is in a state of grief, they are usually emotionally torn. Their communication patterns become a lot different from the way they would have been under normal circumstances. Recognizing a person's grief will help you connect with them in a moment like this.

2. Rage

Rage is at the extreme end of anger, and it is important that you recognize this because knowing the signs can help you take actions that will protect you from the negative outcome. When you are confronted by a person who is enraged, and you recognize this, you are in a better position to decide on how you are going to respond to this. In some cases, it is better to seek protection than take physical action yourself, as this might further enrage the person.

3. Pain

In this situation, I am referring to more than just physical pain. Sometimes the pain that we feel is emotional. When you interact with a person, without realizing it, you might hurt said person. If you are unable to read this emotion in a person, you will continue in the same line of whatever it was you were doing, which would mean that the person will continue to experience this pain. But if you are emotionally intuitive and able to recognize pain, even when they try to mask it with a smile, you would be able to call yourself to order and prevent a situation that will cause harm to another person.

4. Infatuation

This emotion Is not always easy to recognize in a person at a glance, and I almost did not want to include it here. But from my understanding, a lot of friendships, relationships and situation-ships could have been saved if people recognized this and dealt with it sooner to avoid the complicated situation which arises from this.

5. Anxiety

Anxiety can make us act in weird and crazy ways. When a person is nervous, it usually means that they are not in their element, and this could be for a number of reasons. While recognizing this emotion in a person may not immediately point you towards the source of the problem, it will prompt you to take action that will at least help them calm down.

Emotional Cues Based on FBI Interrogation Techniques

1. Know what is normal

There are certain behaviors that are subconscious and unique to us as individuals. When you see and identify those behaviors, you would understand that they don't necessarily mean anything. To pick up on hidden emotional cues, there's important for you to understand the difference between normal and abnormal mannerisms.

2. Look for clusters

Given everything you have read here so far, you should understand that it is going to take more than a wink or a head scratch to accurately identify an emotion. The mannerisms I listed here can happen on their own and don't necessarily interpret as a specific emotion; however, when you see a cluster of emotional markers happening at the same time, you might want to pay attention to what is going on.

3. Pay attention to the sound of the voice

As I mentioned earlier, our voice pitch holds a strong clue to our true emotions. A person may be acting tough and confident, but if you listen to the timbre of their voice, you will realize that that confidence may just be pure bravado. Now, when I am talking about timbre, I am not referring to the loudness of the voice or the lowness of it. There is a frequency for voice pitch that our emotions tune in on. For example, a person who is very confident is not always the loudest, but there is a certain strength to the sound of their voice.

4. Look for clues about their personality

The first chapter of this book was dedicated to helping you understand the different personalities of people. This is so that you will be able to see things from their point of perspective. When next you meet people, try to pick up on emotional cues by looking out for signs that point towards their personalities. By identifying their personalities, you get a behind the scenes sneak peek into the motives that drive such a person, and by doing so, you would be able to uncover the unspoken words they are saying.

5. Identify the action words

When you are looking for the hidden messages a person might be giving off, focusing on nonverbal clues alone might not be enough. Sometimes, the key to unlocking what their true intentions are lies in the words that they actually speak. These words are usually called action words. For example, if a person says, "I don't feel like reading a book," it is safe to say that this person is somewhat impulsive. The way a person phrases certain words can tell you a lot about what their thinking process is like and what their reactions are.

Reading the Room Accurately

A room has a way of determining the emotional outcome of the people in that space is for this reason that it is important whenever you get into a social setting to make an effort to read the room there are several ways to go about this, but in this chapter,

I am only going to focus on three.

1. Take a cue from the invitation card

If the card says the formal event, it simply means that the expected behavior for everyone in such a setting unless indicated otherwise is to dress and act professionally in a professional environment. If you are unsure as to what the atmosphere in the room is going to be like, the invitation card will always provide the right social cues for you.

2. Mirror the actions of people in this space

Paying close attention to the mood and reaction of people in the space can help you read the room better. If your objective is to blend in with the rest of the crowd, reflecting the atmosphere will ensure that you did not stand out awkwardly if your purpose is to socialize, mirroring actions or the mood will help guide your conversation, which would yield better communication.

3. Ask questions and observe

Just because you read a book on reading people doesn't mean that automatically you are going to be able to figure everything out in one go. Sometimes, the best way to get the answers you are looking for is to just ask the questions. Making assumptions and avoiding those questions can lead you to the wrong conclusions. When you are at the wrong end of the stick in a conversation, chances are you will get the boot.

How to Stop Yourself from Acting Under the Influence of Your Emotions

Emotions are a very critical part of our existence as humans. However, if we allow them to dictate our actions, especially when it comes to communications, it could lead us down the wrong path. When you are making an attempt to read a person, you have to try to be objective because putting your emotions in the mix could seriously cloud your judgment and affect your ability to separate between actual reality and your perception of reality. Don't get me wrong; your emotions are a part of you, so I am not asking you to deaden yourself on the inside. I am only saying that you need to learn how to take out your emotions from the equation in order to accurately read a person's body language and facial expressions. How do you do this?

1. Calm yourself down

When you are emotionally excited, there are a lot of thoughts, feelings, and things going on in your head at the same time. You need to clear that space, in order to make way for objectivity, and to do this, the standard calm yourself down routine will be perfect. Just find a way to tune out those emotions or sort through them before dealing with people.

2. Create a mental filter

Before arriving at a conclusion about a person, you need to create a mental filter that sieves through your personal opinions, intuitive analysis, and then rational reasoning. Ask yourself the right questions to determine your reason for coming to that conclusion. If it is anything less than objective analysis, that conclusion might not be right.

3. Concentrate on facts

There are two ways your emotions work for/against you in the process of trying to read people. The first is that it could make you focus on the wrong things just because you are determined to support your own narrative. The second is that it could blind you to serious issues that could negatively impact your relationships further down the line. The easiest way to avoid this is to keep your focus on what is real. Don't just look at one mannerism and draw a conclusion from there. You need to look at the sequence of actions, the social conditions as well as other factors that may influence the person's behavior before coming to a conclusion.

Exercises

The exercises in this chapter are things that you can do every other week or so. It is designed to help you develop self-awareness when it comes to your emotions. Being a good judge of character requires you to have a strong handle on your own emotions. But more than that, it is also about identifying emotions in other people and knowing what to do in situations where you are confronted with certain emotions, especially the ones that make you feel uncomfortable.

1. Take out ten cards and write out ten different emotions on them. Put them inside a bag or a place where you cannot see what is written down on them. Now, randomly pick out two cards from this mix and carry on with the rest of the instructions.

2. List the two cards in front of you and try to answer the following questions as best as you can. Have you ever experienced any of those emotions at any point in your life? If yes, what memory do you have of a moment where you experienced that emotion intensely? What did it take for you to get to that point? If

no, what do you think those two emotions will look like if you find them in a person? Write down your answers.

3. Continue this exercise until you have exhausted all the cards in the bag. Then, repeat the process again with ten new motions. The more you familiarize yourself with these varying emotions, the better you would become at reading them.

Chapter Eleven

PUBLIC SPEAKING WITHOUT FEAR

I remember the first time I ever went on stage to speak in front of a crowd. It was a work event, and being the leading salesperson in the team; I was asked to give a talk to the rest of the staff about how I was able to achieve what I had. I remember getting up there and nearly suffocating myself with sweat and all those feelings of anxiety. I gave the talk, but for the life of me, I cannot remember what it is I said there. The only thing I know for sure is that I lost my audience within the first two minutes of being on stage. It was then I understood the public speaking is not just about having the courage to go on stage. It is also about reading your audience, and in this chapter, I will teach you how to do just that.

Interacting with Your Audience

For the longest time, I used to think that public speaking was a monologue where one person went on stage and droned on and on about something, they are good at or some product they think is very good. But as I continued to participate in public speaking, I realized it is a dialogue that perfectly illustrates the role that non-verbal language plays in our day-to-day communication. The truth of the situation is, in public speaking, one person is actually doing the verbal part of the communication while the audience is communicating non-verbally.

In other words, there are things your audience is saying to you as a public speaker, and if you are able to grasp and understand those things, you become more effective at passing the message across to them and meeting them at the point of their need. The purpose of any conversation is to come to a place of understanding. When you go on stage, and you are so focused on the thing that you want to say that you fail to take into account the opinions or needs of the audience, your speaking event is going to have the same impact as a person who talks to the wall.

One person being able to connect with 1000 people at once without having to talk to them individually is what public speaking is about. That flow of conversation between the speaker and the audience is key to having a successful speaking event. That said, it is important that you prepare for your meetings and events. This way, you have a well thought out message that you are supposed to share with your audience. But when you get on stage, your focus is not just delivering the message. It is ensuring that you are able to give feedback to your audience based on what they are giving you. Waiting till the end of your talk for the Q&A session is not sufficient because the questions you get at that moment is basically from one person's perspective. You need to be able to read your audience and engage them better so as to get the right result from them.

5 Tips for Speaking Publicly Online or Offline

1. Prepare the message with your audience in mind

The message that you have should not be just for or about you. Think of the people who will be attending the event. Try as much as possible to be diverse in your thinking process so that you include the various groups of people and then understand why they would be coming to your event. When you write your message from this perspective, you are able to create content that helps you connect better with them.

2. Dress the part

When you called on to address a group of people, it is because you have been qualified for that part. So, getting on stage requires you to pay attention to this detail. For example, if you have been called upon to talk about success in a specific field, your dressing should speak of success. It doesn't mean you should be extravagant or flamboyant in your outfit. However, maintaining that simple yet elegant look wouldn't hurt that successful image you are trying to project. A bonus from ensuring that you dress the part is the confidence that it gives you.

3. Make good use of space

When you get on stage, one mistake you should try not to make is to create a comfort zone and stick to it. What happens in this situation is that you find yourself standing on one specific spot and doing the talking from there. This does not work well when you are having nonverbal communication given to you. You don't need to pace back and forth aimlessly. But every now and then, take a few steps. Use your hands to gesture and illustrate. Don't exaggerate movement but try to act as if you were having a conversation with just one person, even if there are many people in front of you

4. Use your strong voice

Some people mistake a strong voice for a loud voice. You don't want to do this on stage. Instead, recognize that you are speaking from a place of authority and work with this. When you have this at the back of your mind, that knowledge injects confidence into your voice, and this enables you to project audibly to your audience without needing to shout. But most importantly, it also instills confidence in your audience regarding your abilities.

5. Make eye contact

Now, this can be very scary, especially if you are an introvert who would rather attempt to fly a plane than put themselves out there. But here is a trick I learned; you have to make it seem as though you are looking at one person in the audience when in reality, you are simply picking a spot in the audience and looking at it occasionally. To manage my space on stage well, I try to pick five different spots so that when I am speaking, I am either looking at the message in front of me, the projector screen (if there is one), and any of these five spots in the audience. This way, the people in the audience feel as though I am connecting with them.

Growing Your Self-Confidence

Public speaking is a daunting task for anyone, especially the introvert. One reason I struggled with it was that I felt very shy and lacked confidence; I felt I needed to talk to a group of people. When I was called to speak to my colleagues for the first time about my success as a salesperson, the major issue I knew I had was this thing I would later be able to identify as an impostor syndrome. Basically, you feel like you are not qualified for the success or thing you are being recognized for. I was ready to convince myself that my success was just pure luck and not attributed to my skills and talents as well as my hard work. Thankfully, I had a manager who had excellent people management skills. He understood this about me and encouraged me to push myself past my comfort zone.

To grow your confidence as a public speaker, you need to find the courage to push yourself past your comfort zone, and one of the things I think was instrumental to this process for me was encouraging myself to identify with my successes. Another major ingredient that drowns confidence is a failure to see success or capability in yourself. When you push past this and really see the things you have achieved and give yourself credit for the work you have put into that process, you can build confidence. The confidence that you get from this is not attached to fickle things. It is attached to the person you are, making it more potent and sustainable over time.

In addition to the two things, I have talked about so far, here are some of the things I feel can make a difference in helping you grow your confidence as a public speaker.

1. Be prepared for your speech

2. Use positive words to affirm your abilities and confidence

3. Practice your speech before you go on stage in front of a mirror

4. Doing some physical exercises to pump up your adrenaline a few hours before you go on stage

5. Don't take yourself too seriously.

Using Body Language to Amplify Your Voice

When speaking on stage, it is not just about what you say. It is about how you say it. Being off the Ball to your audience is important if you want to effectively pass your message across. However, your audibility on stage has more to do with the way you walk the stage and use your body language. In this segment, I am going to give you a quick rundown of the things you can do to amplify your voice and the message you want the audience to hear.

1. Speak slowly but steadily

Your speech's rhythm should not be so fast that your audience cannot grasp what you are saying. Calm yourself down, pace yourself and let your rhythm be slow enough to maintain a conversation but not so slow that it feels as if you are reading them a nursery rhyme.

2. Stand tall

When you are in a slouchy position, it minimizes your stage presence and makes you seem smaller than you already are. It doesn't matter how tall or how short you are; holding yourself with confidence can help project your voice's sound. This is more of a visual thing than an audio thing. When you stand tall, your voice sounds stronger and clearer.

3. Free up your arms and legs

Standing stiff in one place is not the best idea if you want to amplify your voice. This is because your stationary position will distract from the message you are trying to pass across. This is ironic because you would think something standing still allows you to focus on every other thing, but because of the nonverbal interaction you are having with the audience, it makes a loud statement about your nervousness and anxiety, and this would drown out everything else you are trying to say.

4. Hide those nervous ticks

While I encourage you to move around, it is important that you ensure the movements are deliberate and conscious as opposed to those nervous mannerisms that come to play when you are feeling anxious. Flapping your arms around aimlessly is almost as bad as standing still in one place. When you move, project yourself as someone who is on a mission, someone who knows exactly what they are doing and is taking calculated steps in the direction of their goals.

5. Inject emotion in your voice and face

Public speaking is not something that robots will be able to do in the future. I believe this is because of the machine's inability to inject emotions into the voice that allows them to connect with their audience. Emotions, in this instance, have very little to do with anger, fear, love, happiness, or what have you. Instead, it is about passion. People need to hear the passion that drives your voice, and for you to sound passionate about what you are saying, you have to believe in it. This is very key to amplifying your voice and connecting with the people listening to you.

Exercise

This particular exercise is targeted at helping you achieve focus and stay relaxed if you have an opportunity to speak to a group of people. It doesn't matter if it is for a wedding event, an office gig, or an actual public space where you be speaking to random strangers; this technique will help you relax almost immediately.

Step one

Find a space where you can sit. It could be on a chair or a mat. Make sure whatever it is you choose is comfortable enough for you.

Step two

Sit in this area you have designated for yourself. Ensure that your spine is straight and your neck is aligned with your spine. Lift your head so that it is facing directly in front of you, not looking above or below the straight line.

Step three

When you have achieved a perfect posture, imagine your muscles relaxing. Let the tension out of your system. Don't hold on to the anxiety. Will yourself to relax.

Step four

Take a deep breath through your nose and hold it for 5 to 10 seconds. Feel the air saturating your tummy as it expands and then exhales through your mouth.

Step five

Repeat this breathing technique for 10 to 15 minutes or until you feel completely relaxed. This deep breathing method has been known to ease anxiety, slow down your breathing pace and help you clear your mind.

Chapter Twelve

THE SUBTLE LANGUAGE OF TOUCH

I could not think of a better way to wrap up this chapter than to focus on an aspect of communication that can be both sensitive and powerful at the same time. It has been a source of a lot of controversies over the years, especially when it comes to communication between members of the opposite sex. I figured that by laying out the ground rules that have to do with this particular form of communication, you are able to better interpret certain gestures and, most importantly, define the boundaries in relationships. The subject matter for this chapter is called touch, and then in a few short moments, I will explain how people use this in communication.

How People Speak with Their Hands

The truth is, our hands play a very vital role in communication without us even realizing it. With your hands, you can say something very sinister to someone. With those same hands, you could flirt up a storm, and with a little extra hand movement, you could make a person feel loved and cared for. With those hand signals ranging across varying emotions, how can you determine what means what in the world of hands speak?

1. Fidgeting

Fidgeting with your hands is any indication that you are feeling insecure or anxious. When you are experiencing these emotions, your brain immediately sends a signal to get your body to calm down, and your hands are usually one of the first to respond to this call. You will find yourself touching your hair, your face, your clothing, or any other object that is within reach.

2. Tapping

This is usually a sign of impatience. When you have reached your emotional limit but are trying to subconsciously hold your peace, you would find yourself tapping your fingers. It is also important to know the person who continuously taps their fingers in a slow and deliberate way is on the verge of making a decision.

3. Covering

Using your hand to cover a specific area of your body could indicate vulnerability. For example, a person covering their wrist with their palm could indicate that they feel remorseful about something they did. When they use their palm to cover their mouth, though, it could be a gesture to indicate that they are trying to hold themselves from saying something or perhaps already said something that they regret

4. Clasped hands or hidden hands

Clasped hands indicate false confidence. They may be trying to project an aura of assurance but in reality, that gesture says this person is not as confident as they said they are. Hidden hands, on the other hand (pun intended), like putting your hands in your pocket, might be sending the message that the person has something to hide.

5. Actual touching

When you touch a person with your fingertips, it is a sign of aggression, especially when you do it forcefully. However, when you lay your hand on the person gently, it could be an indication that you want to bond with the person.

Handshakes and Their True Hidden Meaning

Remember the saying, "the *first impression lasts the longest*"? Well, there are several ways to make a first impression, and in this segment, we are going to focus on one of such ways, which is the handshake. The handshake is what you give a person when you meet them for the first time or in a social setting when you are introducing yourself. It can also be used to affirm the bonds that you share with a person. The way you shake a person's hand passes a strong message about your personality. We are going to look at the three types of handshakes here, although there are several. You could carry out further studies to understand those handshakes.

The Boardroom Handshake

People in positions of power use the boardroom handshake to affirm their power over you. It involves a strong and firm handshake and then using the other hand to grip the forearm of the person. This form of a handshake only lasts less than 3 seconds, but it effectively passes the message across.

The Empathetic Handshake

Sometimes, words are not enough to convey the emotions that you feel, and so, a handshake or other gestures are used to supplement the words. An empathetic handshake is one of those types of gestures. A person who is trying to express their empathy will shake your hand and then use the second hand to cover your hand as a sign to show that they sympathize with you. Again, timing and the circumstances leading up to this are important here. Where negative emotions like grief and pain are being experienced, that hand over your hand might last for less than 5 seconds. However, if the hand stays on for more than 5 seconds, it can make the recipient of that handshake feel very uncomfortable, especially if there is no actual relationship established between the two parties involved.

The Limp Lettuce Handshake

As the name implies, a limp lettuce handshake is a limp handshake lacking in interest, confidence, or any other emotion that might inspire you to consider the person who presented such a handshake in a positive light. At best, that person is simply socially awkward. In a worst-case scenario, there is absolutely no confidence or interest in carrying on the conversation by this person.

What a Person Reveals When They Touch Their Face

One of the most common places we touch when communicating is our face. If you are able to connect these gestures to the conversation you are having, you might be able to peer behind the mental curtains and see what this person is really thinking or feeling.

1. Palm on the forehead

The palm on the forehead gesture indicates disagreement. This person may be subconsciously reacting to something that is being said that they strongly disagree with. Perhaps they may not be in a position to verbally announce their disagreement. However, their subconscious reaction to the statement is so strong that their hands actually speak for them. If this is accompanied by a head shake, you know that this person is definitely not going with the plan or what is being discussed.

2. Finger to the temple

This is one of those times where the expression is not in the "what" that is being done but in the "how" they are doing it. For example, if the person is tapping their temple, it could be an indication that they are exasperated with whatever it is you are saying but are trying to maintain an appearance of interest. Look out for facial expressions that support this, like arched eyebrows. On the other hand, if the person holds one finger to their temple, they might actually be considering what you are saying. But it also speaks to the fact that they are not entirely in agreement with you.

3. Finger on the lips

When a person puts their finger on their lips outrightly, it means you should shut up, and this gesture is considered rude. That being said, there are subconscious ways they might be telling you to keep quiet without necessarily going through this route. For example, if they connect their index fingers and put this over their lips while the other fingers are connected below or above the connected index fingers, it could mean that you are talking too much, and they are internally hoping that you keep quiet.

Exercise

Now that we have come to the last chapter of the book, I am hoping that you were able to get these three messages.

1. You are a very important part of whatever relationships you have with people.

2. You need to be emotionally level-headed in order to detect emotions and other people accurately.

3. The feedback you receive is sometimes built on the energy that you give.

Having this at the back of your mind, let us look at the things you can do to help you become socially acceptable

1. Define the personality you want to project when you meet people

I am not saying you should create a whole new persona entirely because of this exercise. But take your time to list out your areas of strength and talk about how you would like this to be projected to the people you meet. This will help you define the body language that you speak whenever you are in public.

2. Do a before analysis of your body language

Right after you read about specific body language in this book, what were those things you did that projected the wrong perspective about you to people? Before you start working on those gestures, perhaps it would be better to look into why you feel that way and work on changes that would naturally inspire a more positive self-perspective.

3. Give yourself daily tasks

Everything that you learn here can only become effective if you make it a part of your daily routine. Don't leave the knowledge trapped in your mind. Put it to work. Get out there. Mingle. Observe. Learn. Grow.

CONCLUSION

I am glad that you were able to make it from the very first page of this book to this point where the knowledge you have been here will gradually become a reality for you. But I want you to understand that this book does not even begin to touch the surface of the hidden meanings behind human gestures and other forms of non-verbal communication. There is so much that is being said by the people around us that one book and 12 chapters cannot adequately capture. If you are really interested in getting to understand people more, you need to expand your knowledge to other books and research materials conducted by experts.

However, the information you have gotten here will lay an excellent foundation that will serve you in the years to come. If you put the knowledge, I have shared with you to practice; you would be able to experience significant improvements in the way and manner in which you communicate with people. For starters, you would learn how to make yourself more approachable, and then you would also learn how to make people feel at ease around you. It is only when people have some kind of trust and confidence in you that they are able to let down their guard and reveal their true thoughts and intentions to you. And if you ever get the chance to gain someone's trust, it is important that you strive to keep it because once trust is broken, it can almost never be regained.

I am truly honored that you chose to take this journey with me. I hope that some of my experiences that I shared in this book will be able to inspire you to break the barriers that hold you back from living your best life. But most importantly, I hope that you were able to grasp the single lesson of how important you are in any relationship or situation. I wish you the very best on your journey and hope to hear of your exploits and achievements when it comes to transforming your lives as well as the lives of the people that you meet positively. The world needs a lot of positive news right now, but who better to bring that extra dose of positivity into your life than yourself? Once again, thank you for coming with me on this journey. This is me signing out and wishing you a fantastic process on your journey!

REFERENCES

21 common body language mistakes even smart people make. (2016, May 3). Retrieved December 3, 2020, from https://www.businessinsider.com/21-common-body-language-mistakes-even-smart-people-make-2016-4?IR=T#-18

In-text citation

Ackerman, C. M. E. (2020, September 1). 13 Emotional Intelligence Activities & Exercises. Retrieved December 3, 2020, from https://positivepsychology.com/emotional-intelligence-exercises/

Bariso, J. (2020, February 6). An FBI Agent Shares 9 Secrets to Reading People. Retrieved December 3, 2020, from https://www.inc.com/justin-bariso/an-fbi-agents-9-ways-to-read-people.html

Barnard, D. (2018, September 6). How to speak with confidence in public. Retrieved December 3, 2020, from https://virtualspeech.com/blog/speak-with-confidence-in-public

Body Language: Picking Up and Understanding Nonverbal Signals. (n.d.). Retrieved December 3, 2020, from https://www.mindtools.com/pages/article/Body_Language.htm

Buller, A. (2020, April 23). The 7 Types of Handshake and How to Manage Them. Retrieved December 3, 2020, from https://gulfbusiness.com/the-7-types-of-handshake-and-how-to-manage-them/

(c) Copyright skillsyouneed.com 2011-2020. (n.d.). Body Language, Posture and Proximity | SkillsYouNeed. Retrieved December 3, 2020, from https://www.skillsyouneed.com/ips/body-language.html

Phillips, B. (2019, December 5). Three Physical Exercises to Help Reduce Your Speaking Anxiety. Retrieved December 3, 2020, from https://www.throughlinegroup.com/2018/06/24/three-physical-exercises-to-help-reduce-your-speaking-anxiety/

CPSIA information can be obtained
at www.ICGtesting.com
Printed in the USA
LVHW080831191122
733588LV00017B/1405